NGOs and Corporations

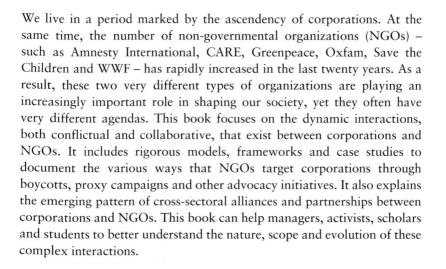

D0068233

We live in a period marked by the ascendency of corporations. At the same time, the number of non-governmental organizations (NGOs) – such as Amnesty International, CARE, Greenpeace, Oxfam, Save the Children and WWF – has rapidly increased in the last twenty years. As a result, these two very different types of organizations are playing an increasingly important role in shaping our society, yet they often have very different agendas. This book focuses on the dynamic interactions, both conflictual and collaborative, that exist between corporations and NGOs. It includes rigorous models, frameworks and case studies to document the various ways that NGOs target corporations through boycotts, proxy campaigns and other advocacy initiatives. It also explains the emerging pattern of cross-sectoral alliances and partnerships between corporations and NGOs. This book can help managers, activists, scholars and students to better understand the nature, scope and evolution of these complex interactions.

MICHAEL YAZIJI is Professor of Strategy and Organizations at IMD and is the Director of the Forum on Corporate Sustainability Management.

JONATHAN DOH is the Herbert G. Rammrath Chair in International Business, founding Director of the Center for Global Leadership, and Associate Professor of Management at the Villanova School of Business.

Business, Value Creation, and Society

Series editors

R. Edward Freeman, University of Virginia
Stuart L. Hart, Cornell University and University of North Carolina
David Wheeler, Dalhousie University, Halifax

The purpose of this innovative series is to examine, from an international standpoint, the interaction of business and capitalism with society. In the twenty-first century it is more important than ever that business and capitalism come to be seen as social institutions that have a great impact on the welfare of human society around the world. Issues such as globalization, environmentalism, information technology, the triumph of liberalism, corporate governance, and business ethics all have the potential to have major effects on our current models of the corporation and the methods by which value is created, distributed, and sustained among all stakeholders – customers, suppliers, employees, communities and financiers.

Published titles:

Fort *Business, Integrity and Peace*
Gomez and Korine *Entrepreneurs and Democracy*
Crane, Matten and Moon *Corporations and Citizenship*
Painter-Morland *Business Ethics as Practice*

Forthcoming titles:

Rivera *Business and Public Policy*

Advance praise

"No major multinational today can ignore NGOs or the tremendous threats and opportunities they represent. With this book, Yaziji and Doh have provided the authoritative volume on the topic, filled with insights and illustrative case studies. I highly recommend it."

Peter Brabeck-Letmathe, Chairman of the Board, Nestlé SA

"This book is the most comprehensive and insightful book on NGOs and NGO-corporations to date. It is essential reading for executives, students and thought leaders wanting to make sense of the rise of NGOs and to better understand how to respond to them."

Antony Burgmans, Former Chairman and CEO, Unilever

"From environmental groups to social justice activists to consumer advocates, NGOs have become critical stakeholders with important business strategy impacts for almost every industry and every company. In *NGOs and Corporations*, Yaziji and Doh map this terrain with breadth and insight . . . a must-read for corporate leaders everywhere."

Dan Esty, Hillhouse Professor, Yale University

"*NGOs and Corporations* is a comprehensive, thoughtful and well-grounded contribution to an important and timely topic. It is a valuable contribution to the evolving literature on NGOs and, particularly, their complex relationships with business firms."

Stephen J. Kobrin, William Wurster Professor of Multinational Management, The Wharton School, University of Pennsylvania

"A useful and comprehensive analysis of the complex and changing relationships between corporations and NGOs."

Sir Mark Moody-Stuart, Chairman of Anglo-American and ex-chairman of Royal Dutch Shell

"This book fills an important gap in our understanding of an increasingly important dimension of business-society relations. Its case studies and analytical framework provide a valuable overview of the dynamics of NGO-firm conflict and cooperation."

David Vogel, Solomon P. Lee Distinguished Professorship in Business Ethics, Stanford University

"No global business executive can afford to ignore or not fully understand NGOs in the twenty-first century. Yaziji and Doh have written a seminal book that helps to explain the unique nature of NGOs and provides an excellent how-to approach to collaborating effectively with them. It is a must-read for any truly global business executive."

Michael D. White, Vice Chairman, PepsiCo

NGOs and Corporations

Conflict and Collaboration

MICHAEL YAZIJI

and

JONATHAN DOH

CAMBRIDGE
UNIVERSITY PRESS

CAMBRIDGE UNIVERSITY PRESS
Cambridge, New York, Melbourne, Madrid, Cape Town, Singapore, São Paulo, Delhi

Cambridge University Press
The Edinburgh Building, Cambridge CB2 8RU, UK

Published in the United States of America by Cambridge University Press, New York

www.cambridge.org
Information on this title: www.cambridge.org/9780521686013

© Michael Yaziji and Jonathan Doh 2009

First published 2009

Printed in the United Kingdom at the University Press, Cambridge

A catalogue record for this publication is available from the British Library.

ISBN 978-0-521-86684-2 hardback
ISBN 978-0-521-68601-3 paperback

The writing of this book was done under very intense professional and personal conditions. (This meant that Jonathan needed to be exceptionally patient with me! Thank you, Jonathan!) I dedicate this book to those whom I love dearly, who have suffered my idiocies, who have supported me during the toughest times and who have given meaning and joy to my life. Thank you for your friendship, guidance, support, light and love. Let's look to the future with levity, optimism and a smile.

MY

I would like to thank my supportive family and all of my friends and colleagues who have helped me along the way, especially Hildy Teegen, without whom my ability to contribute to an effort such as this would not have been possible. I also thank the incredible and talented Michael Yaziji for inviting me to be part of this project.

JPD

Contents

Figures

Tables

Preface

Nonprofit nongovernmental organizations (NGOs) have become important actors in the global political, social, economic and business environment. NGOs – such as Amnesty International, CARE, Greenpeace, Oxfam, Save the Children, World Wide Fund for Nature and hundreds of others – engineer campaigns with the goal of advancing specific causes. Many of these same groups provide goods and services to ameliorate intractable social and environmental problems. Recent statistics indicate a 400 percent increase in the number of international NGOs.[1] Through their advocacy and service delivery, social purpose NGOs work on multiple issues including combating hunger, curtailing human rights abuses, countering environmental degradation and improving health care.

Increasingly, corporations encounter NGOs as the scope of activities among governments, businesses and nonprofits converge. This is reflected, for example, in the twenty-fold increase in citations of "NGOs" or "nongovernmental organizations" in the *Wall Street Journal* and the *Financial Times* in the last ten years.[2]

In some instances, the relationship between NGOs and corporations is antagonistic. NGOs, through campaigns targeting corporations, are not only pushing firms to meet existing social expectations and legal requirements, but also seeking to change broader expectations about corporate responsibility and government regulation.[3] By undermining the firm's legitimacy with key stakeholders, NGOs can erode a firm's market value, destroy its brand, destabilize employee morale, constrain its influence with various constituencies and limit its scope for strategic action. Using a wide range of tactics with different audiences, NGOs increasingly push their agendas – be it the reduction of negative externalities generated by corporations or the wholesale re-evaluation of the corporate capitalistic system – through campaigns targeting corporations.

Simultaneously, NGOs and corporations are also developing more collaborative relationships on the assumption that these connections can yield benefits for both the corporate and NGO participants and the general welfare of the populations of concern to the NGO.[4] These relationships provide corporations with access to different resources, competencies and capabilities than those that are otherwise available within their organizations or that might result from alliances with for-profit organizations.[5] Interestingly, the particular resources and competencies that NGOs bring to a cross-sector partnership are often just what those firms need to address the growing demands of an increasingly diverse set of stakeholders. Similarly, NGOs may be in a position to access financial and nonfinancial resources and expertise from those corporations with whom they collaborate, including managerial and technical skills, marketing leverage and other capabilities.[6]

The impressive complementarities of NGOs and corporations that yield these benefits of partnering are, unfortunately, often accompanied by differences that make these partnerships especially hazard-strewn. First, corporations may need to provide the NGOs with sensitive information. Knowledge about R&D projects, strategic plans and internal audits may help NGOs be better partners, but it may also make them riskier ones. Second, media coverage of the partnership, while potentially beneficial to the reputation of the firm, may put the legitimacy of the NGO under question (as the NGO might be seen as "selling out") and increase the scrutiny of the firm. Finally, there are often cultural diversities and value differences between corporations and NGOs that they must conquer for the partnership to be successful. Corporations are highly focused on the markets and market competition. By contrast, NGOs live and die with shifts in the values and trends of society, as their main foci are on social, political, cultural and environmental issues.

Increasingly, interactions between NGOs and corporations are multidimensional, incorporating both elements of conflict and cooperation. For example, NGOs have been actively pressuring corporations – either individually or through industry-wide campaigns – while at the same time providing technical assistance, such as codes of conduct, standards or other policies and practices, to help corporations respond to the pressure.[7] NGOs have also been active in the explosion of socially responsible investment, an important phenomenon that influences corporate behavior by excluding or including investment holdings based on the social or environmental performance of a company and by pressuring corporations through proxy proposals.[8]

The importance and impact of corporate–NGO engagements – both adversarial and collaborative – is growing. A fuller understanding of the role of business in society requires a comprehensive understanding of these engagements. To date, most of the work done in the area has been limited to descriptive case studies, with few efforts to provide a more comprehensive typology and theoretical framework for understanding these engagements. We seek to fill some of these gaps.

This is the first full-length volume to systematically examine these emerging relationships. Our objective in writing this book is to inform both managerial theory and practice related to the forces driving the emergence of relationships between NGOs and corporations. In doing so, we will examine the nature, scope and evolution of these relationships over time, with the objectives of:

1. Explaining why NGOs have emerged as important institutional and organizational actors on the global political–economic landscape.
2. Developing, synthesizing and presenting typologies of NGOs to help the reader gain a better understanding of their position in the broader political and economic environment and to differentiate the purpose, mission, organization and operation between and among various types of NGOs.
3. Explaining the range of ways in which corporations and NGOs interact, including NGO campaigns, corporate–NGO collaborations and other engagements.
4. Describing and documenting different types of NGO campaigns, including boycotts, media initiatives, shareholder resolutions and other tactics.
5. Describing and documenting the range of ways in which corporations and NGOs compete and collaborate, including via philanthropic contributions, formal and informal agreements, codes of conduct and standards, and other mechanisms.
6. Documenting the dynamics of corporate–NGO relationships as they evolve from conflicting to cooperative relationships through exploration of critical case studies.

7. Discussing the emerging role of NGOs in the broader field of business and society.

In sum, we hope this volume makes a timely and innovative contribution to the literature on business and society and the growing importance of NGOs within that field. By offering a succinct, straightforward and sophisticated treatment of this important and emerging issue in global business and society, we hope that our contribution has the potential to change the way scholars, educators and practitioners think about this important topic.

Notes

1 M. Yaziji, "Turning gadflies into allies," *Harvard Business Review*, February (2004), 110–115.
2 M. Yaziji, "Institutional change and social risk: A study of campaigns by social movement organizations against firms," INSEAD (2004).
3 J. P. Doh and H. Teegen (eds.), *Globalization and NGOs: Transforming Business, Government, and Society* (Westport: Praeger, 2003).
4 H. Teegen, J. P. Doh and S. Vachani, "The importance of nongovernmental organizations (NGOs) in global governance and value creation: An international business research agenda," *Journal of International Business Studies* 35 (6) (2004), 463–483.
5 Yaziji, "Turning gadflies," 110–115.
6 J. W. Selsky and B. Parker, "Cross-sector partnerships to address social issues: Challenges to theory and practice," *Journal of Management* 31 (2005), 849–873; Teegen, Doh and Vachani, "The importance of nongovernmental organizations," 463–483.
7 J. P. Doh and T. R. Guay, "Globalization and corporate social responsibility: How nongovernmental organizations influence labor and environmental codes of conduct," *Management International Review* 44 (3) (2004), 7–30.
8 T. Guay, J. Doh and G. Sinclair, "Nongovernmental organizations, shareholder activism, and socially responsible investments: Ethical, strategic, and governance implications," *Journal of Business Ethics* 52 (1) (2004), 125–139.

Foreword

This book could not have come at a more propitious time. With the global financial meltdown, sub-prime mortgage mess, collapse of the auto sector and escalating concerns about abrupt climate change, it is clear that "business-as-usual" strategies will simply not suffice. Never has stakeholder engagement and collaboration with civil society been more important. Indeed, the twenty-first century appears to demand nothing less than a new, more inclusive approach to capitalism that promotes "mutual value" for not only companies, customers and suppliers, but also communities and the environment.

Luckily for us, Michael Yaziji and Jonathan Doh provide a welcome roadmap for how to both understand this transformation and to benefit from it competitively. In *NGOs and Corporations* they first explain why non-governmental organizations (NGOs) have exploded onto the scene over the past two decades. They provide a lucid model for both explaining and predicting the emergence of civil society based upon underlying conditions at the national and global level.

Next, the authors provide a classification of NGOs so as to better organize our thinking about the different strategies and types of actors, and the range of ways that corporations and NGOs interact. They make a strong case that "social" risk is now as significant strategically as "political" or "technological" risk. In so doing, they provide a model for predicting which types of firms are most likely to be the target of NGO campaigns of "delegitimation."

Yaziji and Doh also make clear that all NGO campaigns are not created equal. They show, for example, that NGOs serving as "watchdogs" – the enforcement of existing laws and norms – are more likely to employ tactics using dominant institutions such as courts, legislators and regulatory bodies. In contrast, those aiming for change to the central tenets of dominant institutions employ "counter-institutional" tactics, including civil disobedience, destruction of property and violence as tactics to achieve their aims. Indeed, they suggest that al Qaeda represents one of the most successful "radical" NGOs in the world today employing "counter-institutional" tactics.

The book greatly benefits from a number of practical cases and illustrations which bring the analytical and conceptual models to life. These cases range from GMO food, to Coke in India, to conflict diamonds, to Unilever and Oxfam. The cases selected represent not only the full range of NGO-Corporate engagement types, but also provide a wonderful sense of how NGO engagement has evolved and progressed over the past two decades: Historically, NGOs typically employed either a "collaborative" or a "confrontational" strategy; increasingly, however, evidence suggests that more NGOs are using a hybrid or "mixed" strategy, employing collaboration where appropriate but also engaging in confrontation or direct action where necessary.

Finally, the closing chapter of the book reflects upon the "next wave" of corporate-NGO interaction. Here, the globalization of both industry and civil society are discussed, along with the growing importance and emergence of NGOs in the developing world. This last topic is near and dear to me and, in my view, will become increasingly important in the next decade. Indeed, the role of NGOs in helping to create a sustainable form of development among the four billion poor at the "bottom of the economic pyramid" may turn out to be the most important role for civil society in the coming years.

We are very pleased indeed, to publish this book in the series on *Business, Value Creation, and Society*. The purpose of the series is to stimulate thinking about new ways to combine economic value creation with social contribution and environmental sustainability. Yaziji and Doh have clearly made an important contribution toward this end.

STUART L. HART
S.C. Johnson Chair in Sustainable Global Enterprise
Johnson Graduate School of Management
Cornell University
Ithaca, NY
USA

Acknowledgments

We would both like to acknowledge the support of our families and the academic institutions that constitute our professional home: IMD (Yaziji) and the Villanova School of Business (Doh). We also thank Elizabeth Stewart for helpful research assistance and the team at Cambridge, especially Chris Harrison and Paula Parish, for their encouragement, patience and expert guidance.

PART I

Understanding NGOs

1 | *Classifying NGOs: definitions, typologies and networks*

The business–society interface has changed over the last decades of the twenty-first century as disparate interests within civil society have coalesced around an increasingly vocal – and powerful – nongovernmental or "third" sector. Nongovernmental organizations (NGOs) – the organizational manifestation of this movement – have gained considerable influence in government, business and within broader society. A coherent understanding of NGOs is a necessary precondition for proper consideration not only of their activities and influence, but also of the nature of the corporate–NGO interactions. In this chapter, we provide a definition of NGOs, a typology for conceptualizing the different varieties of NGOs, and discuss the importance of networks and coalitions to NGOs.

Definitions of NGOs

Although the term NGO is relatively recent, associations among like-minded individuals have been part of both ancient and modern history. When Tocqueville first visited the United States, he was struck by the fact that:

Americans of all ages, all stations of life and all types of disposition are forever forming associations... In democratic countries knowledge of how to combine is the mother of all other forms of knowledge; on its progress depends that of all the others. There are not only commercial and industrial associations in which all take part, but others of a thousand different types – religious, moral, serious, futile, very general and very limited, immensely large and very minute... Nothing, in my view, deserves more attention than the intellectual and moral associations in America.[1]

Civil society, also referred to as the "third sector" or the "nonprofit" sector, is used to broadly describe all aspects of society that extend beyond the realm of the public and the private sectors.[2] Unlike state-based

3

membership inherent in citizenship, association in civil society is voluntary, and it is characterized by individuals coalescing around common ideas, needs or causes to promote collective gain. It can be said that once these individuals unite in an organized or semi-organized fashion, they are taking collective action.[3]

When individuals or groups within civil society work together to advance a broad common set of interests, and these interests become a significant force in shaping the direction of society, the outcomes of this process are often called social movements. Social movements can be thought of as broad societal initiatives organized around a particular issue, trend or priority.[4] Modern examples include the environmental movement and the feminist movement.

When civil society groups come together to form more organized relationships, the entities that emerge are often referred to as nongovernmental organizations or NGOs. NGO is a broad term that is used somewhat loosely to refer to all organizations that are neither an official part of government (at any level) nor a private, for-profit enterprise. Within the category, however, there are many different types, characteristics and purposes of NGOs. Vakil suggests that:

[The] lack of consensus on how to define and classify nongovernmental organizations has inhibited progress on both the theoretical and empirical fronts in the effort to better understand and facilitate the functioning of the NGO sector.[5]

The term "nongovernmental organization" dates from 1950, when the United Nations (UN) coined the expression.[6] Presumably the UN, which primarily dealt with governments and wanted to consult private, nonprofit organizations that were independent of governments, found it convenient to refer to them simply as nongovernmental organizations to distinguish them from governments. Today the UN describes an NGO as:

any non-profit, voluntary citizens' group which is organized on a local, national or international level. Task-oriented and driven by people with a common interest, NGOs perform a variety of services and humanitarian functions, bring citizens' concerns to Governments, monitor policies and encourage political participation at the community level. They provide analysis and expertise, serve as early warning mechanisms and help monitor and implement international agreements. Some are organized around specific issues, such as human rights, the environment or health.[7]

Another, more technical definition is offered by Hudson and Bielefeld:

NGOs are organizations that (1) provide useful (in some specified legal sense) goods or services, thereby serving a specified public purpose, (2) are not allowed to distribute profits to persons in their individual capacities, (3) are voluntary in the sense that they are created, maintained, and terminated based on voluntary decision and initiative by members or a board and (4) exhibit value rationality, often based on strong ideological components.[8]

Teegen *et al.* provide a more succinct definition, referring to social purpose NGOs as:

private, not-for-profit organizations that aim to serve particular societal interests by focusing advocacy and/or operational efforts on social, political and economic goals, including equity, education, health, environmental protection and human rights.[9]

NGO typologies

NGOs can be broadly divided along two dimensions – (a) whom the NGO is designed to benefit and (b) what the NGO does. This taxonomy yields the matrix shown in Figure 1.1.

Before looking at these different dimensions, a rather obvious caveat is worth making explicit. The typology depicted in Figure 1.1 is

		Service	Advocacy
Beneficiary	Self	Alcoholics Anonymous Chess clubs	Labor unions Trade associations
	Others	Salvation Army CARE	WWF Amnesty International
		Type of activity	

Figure 1.1 Typology of NGOs

archetypical; in reality a single NGO may occupy more than a single quadrant at any given time and may move from quadrant to quadrant over time.

Who benefits from the NGO?

The first dimension concerns whom the NGO is intended to benefit. NGOs have multiple sets of stakeholders, often including financial contributors, board members, executives, staff and beneficiaries. Obviously, each of these groups of stakeholders can be composed of different types of individuals or organizations and the structure can vary enormously. For example, financial donors could include individuals, private foundations, governments and multilateral institutions; the staff might be comprised of paid workers or volunteers and the board could be executive or non-executive.

Self-benefiting NGOs

Self-benefiting NGOs are often membership associations designed primarily to provide a benefit to their members, generally as a result of pooling interests. They are distinguishable by the fact that the financial and/or labor contributors to the NGO are themselves members of the group of intended beneficiaries. Examples of self-serving NGOs are unions, business associations, church groups, community patrol groups, Alcoholics Anonymous and amateur sports clubs.

Other-benefiting NGOs

By contrast, other-benefiting NGOs are organizations in which the capital and labor contributors are not themselves members of the primary intended beneficiary group; or the pool of beneficiaries is so broad that the public good produced will be shared by a wide swath of society. In other words, the supporters are not donating to gain excludable private goods for themselves or their self-identified group. The World Wildlife Fund (WWF), Greenpeace, Amnesty International, CARE, the Open Society and Doctors Without Borders/Médecins Sans Frontières (MSF) are examples of other-benefiting NGOs.

Some differentiating characteristics

Admitting to generalizations and broad brushstrokes, there are a few interesting characteristics that differentiate self-benefiting and other-benefiting NGOs. Self-benefiting NGOs tend to have a higher level of accountability to their intended recipients. The intended recipients are also the contributors and if the benefits of the NGO seem to be outweighed by the costs of contribution, the NGO will face pressure to improve its performance by its contributors. The primary organizational challenge is to prove efficacy and overcome issues of collective action such as tragedy of the commons and free riding.

By comparison, other-benefiting NGOs tend to have less accountability because they are not as dependent on their beneficiaries for their financial or labor resources. If they fail to serve their beneficiaries efficiently or effectively, but they can convince their contributors otherwise, they can continue to garner the necessary resources. The primary organizational challenge is to inspire and tap into the altruism that is required to gather financial and labor support.

There are some obvious differences that result from these different organizational challenges. Self-benefiting NGOs tend to be seen as instruments of the contributors to gain benefit. While there can be some enthusiasm about the organization among its contributors, often the contributors do not see the organization as serving some higher purpose or of significant value in and of itself. By contrast, other-benefiting NGOs that rely on inspiring and tapping into the altruism of contributors tend to be very value-laden and "inspirational," with contributors being "true believers" in the organization and its purpose.

There is also a noticeable difference in how outside individuals and organizations view self-benefiting and other-benefiting NGOs. In general, the population holds other-benefiting NGOs in high moral regard to the extent that they see these NGOs as selfless workers for the public good. By contrast, self-benefiting NGOs are not held in as high regard, but are instead seen through a skeptical eye if the organization is advocating for its members' own benefits, or simply as "neutral," as in such service organizations as social or sports clubs.

Types of NGO activities

Over time, private sectors have expanded while public sectors have eroded, allowing for NGO sectors to subsequently grow and evolve with the surrounding environment. Figure 1.2 depicts this dynamic in greater detail while highlighting certain outcomes and future concerns regarding NGO activity. Strategic decisions have since brought to

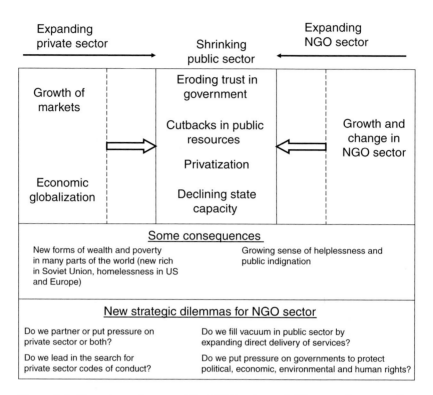

Figure 1.2 Changing private, public, NGO roles and dilemmas for expanding NGO sector (adapted from M. Lindenberg and J. P. Dobel, "The challenges of globalization for northern international relief and development NGOs," *Nonprofit and Voluntary Sector Quarterly* 28 (4) (1999), 13)

light a second dimension distinguishing NGO activities, which can be divided into "advocacy" and "service" sector NGOs.

Advocacy NGOs
Advocacy NGOs work to shape the social, economic or political system to promote a given set of interests or ideology. They engage in lobbying, serve as representatives and advisory experts to decision-makers, conduct research, hold conferences, stage citizen tribunals, monitor and expose actions (and inactions) of others, disseminate information to key constituencies, set/define agendas, develop and promote codes of conduct and organize boycotts or investor actions.

In these ways, advocacy NGOs give voice and provide access to institutions to promote social gain and/or mitigate negative spillovers from other economic activity.

A finer distinction between two types of advocacy NGOs – "watchdog" and "social movement" NGOs – is worth highlighting.

In brief, **watchdog** NGOs are less ideologically radical, relative to the communities in which they operate, and are generally satisfied with the broader economic, legislative, political and social institutions. Thus, the role of watchdog NGOs is not to radically change the system but ensure that the requirements of the system are actually being met by various other organizations, such as firms and regulatory and legislative bodies.

By contrast, **social movement** NGOs are not trying to support the existing system, but to change or undermine it. The more radical the social movement organization, the more radical the change they are pursuing. These topics are covered in more detail in Chapter 4, including further developments on the differences between these two forms of advocacy groups, and greater focus on their disparities regarding campaigns, goals and tactics.

Service NGOs

Service-oriented NGOs provide goods and services to clients with unmet needs. NGOs have long stepped in to serve as critical "safety nets" where politically challenged, indebted or corrupt states are unable or unwilling to provide for societal needs, and where global problems defy the conception of nation-state responsibilities. Examples of such service activities include relief efforts provided by the Red Cross/Red Crescent, natural resources monitoring by WWF and the distribution of medicinal drugs by Doctors Without Borders.

Hybrid and evolving NGOs

As noted above, although some NGOs focus primarily on advocacy or service delivery, many others pursue both sets of activities simultaneously, or evolve from one to the other. For example, Oxfam, the global development and poverty relief organization, advocates for changes in public policy that would provide greater support to its efforts while also contributing directly to health, education and food security in the developing countries in which it operates. Similarly,

Doctors Without Borders and WWF are active on the ground, delivering services in their respective domains, but they also simultaneously lobby in the legislative arenas.

The following brief example on environmental conservation illustrates the relationship among civil society, social movements and the emergence (and convergence) of different types of NGOs. Environmental conservation has long been of concern to civil society in North America. A strong and ongoing conservation movement gave rise to two service-oriented environmental organizations, the Nature Conservancy (founded in 1951) and WWF (founded in 1961). This longstanding movement, in conjunction with a growing social movement and related activism over civil rights and the Vietnam War in the early and mid-1960s, gave rise to the environmental movement of the 1960s.

This movement gained momentum after the publication of Rachel Carson's *Silent Spring*,[10] which exposed the hazards of the pesticide DDT, eloquently questioned humanity's faith in technological progress and helped set the stage for the environmental movement. In turn, this paved the way for the creation of a number of environmental advocacy organizations, such as the Environmental Defense Fund (founded in 1967) and the National Resources Defense Council (founded in 1970). Over time, many environmental advocacy organizations developed more of a service focus, and many service NGOs began to take positions on environmental policy issues, creating some convergence in these organizations and their missions. Figure 1.3 presents a stylized depiction of this evolution.

NGOs and their networks

In the typology discussion above, we considered each NGO in isolation. However, to understand the NGO world, we need to recognize and understand the important role of NGO networks. In a recent review of network theory from a multilevel perspective, Brass *et al.* suggest that social network theory is still relatively underutilized as a theoretical foundation to explain and illuminate organizational phenomena.[11] Doh *et al.* argue that because of their limited resources, diverse goals and competition for support, NGOs are particular beneficiaries of network involvement. They suggest that the types of networks employed, and the relative utility of these network types,

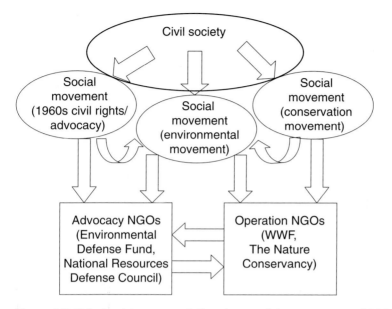

Figure 1.3 Relationship among civil society, social movements and NGOs: the example of the environmental movement

differs for NGOs when compared to networks among private, for-profit corporations. They cite the concepts of power and influence as instruments used by NGO actors to achieve desired outcomes as critical variables to better understand network usage by NGOs. They then develop a typology of NGO network usage based upon (1) network connection locus and (2) network goal scope wherein the instruments of power and influence are activated by these organizations.[12]

Another network approach to NGOs considers them within the context of policy networks – self-organizing groups that coordinate a growing number of public (decision-makers) and private (interest groups) actors for the purpose of formulating and implementing public policies. Policy networks may be viewed as a sub-category of inter-organizational networks, most often defined in terms of their structural characteristics and function. When defined according to their structure, inter-organizational networks can be viewed as "a cluster or

complex of organizations connected to each other by resource
dependencies and distinguished from other clusters or complexes by
breaks in the structure of resource dependencies."[13] From a functional
perspective, inter-organizational networks can be characterized as a
"political economy concerned with the distribution of two scarce
resources – money and authority. Organizations, as participants in the
political economy, pursue an adequate supply of resources."[14] Both
definitions thus stress the central importance of resource exchanges
among network members. What distinguishes policy networks from
other types of inter-organizational networks is that they function to
formulate and implement public policy.[15] Members can include private
actors, academics, public decision-makers, journalists and others;
however, there is no single category of actor that is systematically
present in all types of policy networks.[16]

In practice, there is evidence that NGOs themselves view their
network relationships with affiliates and allies as particularly effective
due to the flexibility and responsiveness of the network. Lindenberg
and Dobel document traditional and evolving global structures for
NGOs as they respond to resource challenges, donor demands and
globalization itself. They argue that NGOs are increasingly likely to
adopt a structure similar to a confederation or federation, versus
looser, independent or unitary corporate models. Here, *confeder-
ations* are structured such that strong members delegate some
coordination, standard-setting and resource allocation duties to the
central office while *federations* are structured such that the center has
strong powers for standard-setting and resource acquisition, but
affiliates have separate boards and implementation capacity. In addition, northern NGOs – those headquartered in the developed world –
are seeking to move from "having largely northern boards and
affiliates with mixed northern and southern staff that gain most
resources from the north" with the goal of creating more global
organizations that draw on the resources of both northern and
southern countries and support programs in both the north and south
involving partners from all parts of the globe.[17] Figure 1.4 provides a
visual spectrum of these models.

In addition to network relationships among affiliates of the same
global organization (e.g. Oxfam USA and Oxfam Great Britain)
and collaborative activities among different NGOs (e.g. WWF and
The Nature Conservancy), there are a number of NGO umbrella

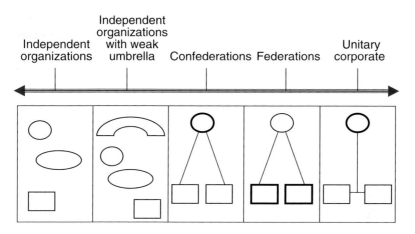

Figure 1.4 Models of north relief and development NGOs (adapted from M. Lindenberg and J. P. Dobel, "The challenges of globalization for northern international relief and development NGOs," *Nonprofit and Voluntary Sector Quarterly* 28 (4) (1999), 15)

organizations – trade associations – that provide opportunities for broader collaboration among NGOs. These include, for example, the Steering Committee on Humanitarian Response (SCHR), InterAction and the International Council of Voluntary Agencies (ICVA).

Conclusion

In this chapter we have attempted to build a foundation of understanding the various types and levels of NGOs. We have provided several definitions that allow for the development of a typology of NGOs with several key dimensions of differentiation. These include what the NGO does ("advocacy" or "service," with "watchdog" versus "social movement" NGOs as subsets of advocacy NGOs) and the relevant beneficiaries of that activity ("self" or "others"). We also discussed the importance of networks and coalitions to NGOs and the accomplishments of their missions. In the following chapter we will delve more deeply into the underlying drivers behind the rise of NGOs.

Notes

1 A. de Tocqueville, *Democracy in America*, translated by George Lawrence (New York: Harper & Row [1835], 1966), pp. 485–488.

2 H. Teegen, J. P. Doh and S. Vachani, "The importance of nongovern-
   mental organizations (NGOs) in global governance and value creation:
   An international business research agenda," *Journal of International
   Business Studies* 35 (6) (2004), 463–483.

3 M. Olson, *The Logic of Collective Action: Public Goods and the Theory
   of Groups*, second printing with new preface and appendix (Cambridge,
   MA: Harvard University Press, 1971).

4 Teegen, Doh and Vachani, "The importance of nongovernmental
   organizations," 463–483.

5 A. Vakil, "Confronting the classification problem: Toward a taxonomy
   of NGOs," *World Development* 25 (12) (1997), 2057.

6 Vakil, "Confronting the classification problem," 2068.

7 United Nations, *Arrangements and Practices for the Interaction of Non-
   Governmental Organizations in All Activities of the United Nations
   System* (New York: Report of the Secretary-General, United Nations,
   1998), para. 1.

8 B. A. Hudson and W. Bielefeld, "Structures of multinational nonprofit
   organizations," *Nonprofit Management and Leadership* 8 (a) (1997), 32.

9 Teegen, Doh and Vachani, "The importance of nongovernmental
   organizations," 466.

10 R. Carson, *Silent Spring* (Boston: Houghton Mifflin, 1962).

11 D. J. Brass, J. Galaskiewicz, H. R. Greve and W. Tsai, "Taking stock of
    networks and organizations: A multilevel perspective," *Academy of
    Management Journal* 47 (6) (2004), 795–817.

12 J. P. Doh, J. Teegen and W. Newburry, "Cooperative strategies in
    environmental NGOs," in J. P. Doh and H. Teegen (eds.), *Globalization
    and NGOs: Transforming Business, Government, and Society* (Westport:
    Praeger, 2003), pp. 65–80.

13 J. K. Benson, "A framework for policy analysis," in D. L. Rogers and
    D. A. Whetten (eds.), *Interorganizational Co-ordination* (Ames: Iowa
    State University Press, 1982), p. 148.

14 J. K. Benson, "The interorganizational network as a political economy,"
    Administrative Science Quarterly 20 (1975), 229–249.

15 B. Marin and R. Mayntz (eds.), *Policy Networks. Empirical Evidence and
    Theoretical Considerations* (Frankfurt: Campus, 1991), p. 16.

16 Marin and Mayntz (eds.), *Policy Networks*, p. 17.

17 M. Lindenberg and J. P. Dobel, "The challenges of globalization for
    Northern international relief and development NGOs," *Nonprofit and
    Voluntary Sector Quarterly* 28 (4) (1999), 16.

2 | *The emergence of NGOs in the context of business–government–societal relationships*

How are we to understand the increasing frequency and impact of interactions between NGOs and corporations? In this chapter, we will investigate the conditions that have favored the significant rise in the number, power and societal influence of NGOs – with a particular focus on advocacy NGOs – in the past two decades. The focus of this chapter will be on the contextual drivers of the rise of the NGO rather than the more motivation-focused approach discussed by others.[1]

NGOs constitute an important and influential set of actors within the broad context of business and society. NGOs have emerged as critical organizations in shaping governmental policy and practice, influencing legal and institutional structures and affecting corporate and business activities. Although NGOs or their equivalents have been part of human societies for centuries, in recent decades, NGOs have grown in number, power and influence. Their force has been felt in a range of major public policy debates, and NGO activism has been responsible for major changes in public policy, law and regulation, and in reforming corporate behavior and governance.[2]

The worldwide NGO presence

Estimates of the number of NGOs vary widely, although almost all analysts agree that the number is dramatically increasing. In 1993, the United Nations Development Program identified 50,000 NGOs worldwide,[3] while the Union of International Associations identified 52,000 such groups worldwide. In 2001, the last year for which complete figures are available, the total size of the "independent sector" (non-firm, nongovernment) in the United States was estimated at 1.4 million organizations, with revenues of nearly $680 billion and an estimated 11.7 million employees.[4] In terms of international development, current estimates indicate that over 15 percent of total overseas development aid is channeled through NGOs. Indeed, a

report published by the UN and the NGO SustainAbility notes that
the global nonprofit sector, with its more than $1 trillion turnover,
could rank as the world's eighth largest economy. For the United
States, in the 1970s, approximately 70 percent of resource flows to the
developing world were from official development assistance and 30
percent were private. In 2003, just 15 percent of $102.5 billion in
resource flows were comprised of direct government assistance, with
85 percent coming from nongovernmental resources, of which 45
percent were private capital flows, 15 percent NGO assistance and 25
percent personal remittances.[5]

Despite differences among estimates, most observers agree that
NGOs are growing in number and importance. As mentioned in the
Preface, there has been a 400 percent increase in international NGOs
over the last decade and, as already indicated, a twenty-fold increase in
the mention of NGOs in the *Financial Times* and *Wall Street Journal*
over this period.[6] According to a 1995 World Bank report,[7] since the
mid-1970s, the NGO sector in both developed and emerging countries
has experienced exponential growth. Hart and Milstein note, "As the
power of national governments has eroded in the wake of global trade
regimes, nongovernmental organizations (NGOs) and other civil society groups have stepped into the breach."[8] Teegen *et al.* propose that
the emergence of civil society in general, and the activism of civic NGOs
in particular, have broad implications for the role, scope and definition
of corporations in the global economy.[9] Doh and Teegen point out that
the emergence of NGOs has, in some cases, supplanted the role of host
governments in the historic business–government bargaining relationship such that NGOs yield significant power over the multinational
enterprise's (MNE's) right to operate in developing countries.[10]

This growth in terms of number, power and influence of NGOs
represents one of the most important societal developments in the past
twenty years, in terms of how the dynamics of public debates and
government policies concerning corporate behavior are changing.[11]
Researchers have noted both the drivers of NGO pressure on corporations,[12] as well as how this pressure can affect corporate behavior.[13]

Conditions conducive to the emergence of NGOs

There are three necessary and collectively sufficient conditions for the
emergence of significant social movements and NGOs. First, there

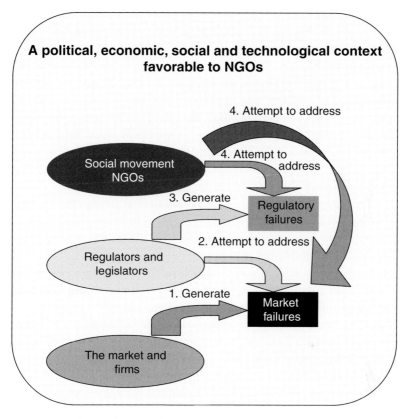

Figure 2.1 The market–regulatory–NGO system

must be dissatisfaction among some segment of the population with some aspect of society, be it social, economic, political or technological. Second, the population must be of the understanding that the existing political processes and structures have not sufficiently addressed this dissatisfaction. Finally, the social, economic, political and technological context must allow for social movement NGOs to be seen as a relatively effective means of addressing the perceived shortcomings.

The basic model shown in Figure 2.1 will provide the structure for the remainder of this chapter. We see that markets and firms are the source of market failures. Regulators and legislators attempt to address these market failures, but when they are unsuccessful, they create regulatory failures. If the political, economic, social and tech-nological conditions are right, NGOs will step in to address both the market and regulatory failures.

Service and advocacy NGOs address these failures in different ways. Service NGOs, as introduced in Chapter 1, attempt to address the consequences of market and regulatory failures by stepping in to provide the services directly to their beneficiaries. For example, Alco-holics Anonymous, the Salvation Army, Doctors Without Borders and the many other service NGOs providing food, shelter, clothing and medical treatment to their beneficiaries all address needs that are not being fully met by the market or the government. Advocacy NGOs, such as Greenpeace, Amnesty International, Sweatshop Watch and others apply pressure to market players, regulators and legislators in order to have these players themselves address the failures and respond in a socially acceptable manner.

As the chapter progresses, we will follow the above logic to explain the incredible rise in NGOs that we have witnessed over the last decade. We will first focus on dissatisfaction with the economic sys-tem and its obvious spillover effects on the social system by distin-guishing the four forms of perceived market failures that have been an impetus for the rise of NGOs. We will then focus on four sources of regulatory failures that give rise to the perception that the dominant political processes and structures, i.e. legislators and regulators, are not adequately addressing societal problems. Finally, we will highlight the social, economic, political and technological conditions that have favored the rise of NGOs in many countries.

Dissatisfaction with the economic system: three forms of market failure

In the developed world, many (with the exception of the most radical social movement NGOs) see the capitalist system and the market as creating a great deal of value and wealth through the "invisible hand" of the price mechanism and the profit-seeking activities of firms. To this extent, they see the capitalist system and the firms that operate within it as beneficial to society. Yet, three forms of perceived "market failures," outlined below, can arise and have serious social, economic or environmental costs; these perceived market failures generate dissatisfaction with the status quo and lead to the initiation of social movements and the rise of NGOs.

Social desirability

A principal market failure that helps give rise to NGO action is when the market will not adequately provide all goods and services that are *socially desirable*.[14] There are goods the market cannot or will not provide because it is simply not profitable to do so. That is, there are cases of human need, where there is no economic demand; there are people in desperate need of basic goods and services who lack the economic means to purchase them. The most obvious examples include lack of food for famine-stricken countries, lack of vaccines for diseases that exclusively afflict developing countries, and lack of availability of existing medicines for the poor in developing countries.

Externalization

Externalization, a second form of market failure, occurs when the price of goods and services do not reflect the true costs of producing those goods and services. In this category, the most perceived obvious market failures concern *environmental* issues such as the use of raw resources or the pollution created when producing or using a product. For example, collapsing fish stocks can be understood to be the result of fishing fleets not paying the full global cost or value of the fish that they are pulling from the sea. Complaints about similar perceived market failures are often aired concerning unsustainable logging practices and strip mining, heavy use of pesticides and water in farming, the use of genetically modified organisms (GMOs) in farming and the CO_2 emissions resulting from the production and use of fossil-fuel-based energy sources. While there are debates about what the true "full cost" is of some of these practices, from a perspective of sustainability, the full cost should be linked to the cost of replacing the used resource (as in the case of fishing, logging, etc.) or returning the environment to its prior state before the pollution-causing activity. For example, the full cost of releasing a ton of CO_2 should be tied to the cost of extracting a ton of CO_2 back out of the environment.

A more contentious version of this type of market failure concerns the *indirect* costs associated with the use of a product or service. For example, arms manufacturers, abortion providers, alcohol producers, tobacco manufacturers, producers and marketers of pornography and using sexually objectifying images of women are often challenged by NGOs because of the indirect costs to society of the use of their products or services. The "market failure" complaint in this case is that third parties who are not given a choice in the matter and who are not compensated absorb some of the costs of the use of the product.

Whether this is truly a form of market failure is up for debate. Some would claim that pornography, advertising of certain forms, use of alcohol and tobacco and violence are all forms of "cultural pollution" and thus a cost that society must bear. Whether these costs can appropriately be squeezed under the label of "market failure" is ultimately a semantic debate; of more significance is that these activities are indeed seen as problematic in and of themselves or as contributing to social or environmental ills.

The power of imperfect competition

The final form of market failure concerns *imperfect competition* and the power that it can provide to one actor over another in a transaction. Monopolies and monopsonies – products or services offered by many sellers only sought by one buyer – are the most obvious form of such market failures. Firms in the preferred positions in these imperfect market structures have negotiating power with their transacting partner that they would not have in perfect competition. Market failures of this kind would include firms paying "unfair" wages to laborers with few outside alternatives or charging "excessive" prices from captive and dependent customers.

Another subset of this form of market failure is not one of power through the imperfect market structure of small numbers of buyers or sellers, but power through *asymmetry of information or influence* of those involved in a transaction. For example, the Baby Milk Action group attacks Nestlé, which the group sees as selling baby milk formula in poor countries to mothers who, if fully informed, would not use the product or would use it differently. Similarly, Commercial Alert, McSpotlight and other NGOs have campaigned against firms that advertise unhealthy snacks as comparable alternatives to easily influenced children.

Dissatisfaction with regulatory and legislative responses to market failures

When markets and states fail to meet society's needs, the question then becomes, what should be done to address these market failures and their consequences and who should do it? Often, the responsibility is seen as residing in the lap of government. Regulation and legislation, it is thought, should address the three forms of market failure discussed above. For example, with regard to the first form of market failure – the market not meeting the needs of those who cannot pay – the modern welfare state is often expected to step in and ensure that basic human needs are met.

In the second form of market failure – externalities – regulators and legislators are often expected to develop regulations that minimize this externalization of costs and address the impact on society of any externalized costs that cannot be effectively or efficiently internalized through legislation. Examples of this type of regulation include restrictions on overfishing of fish stocks, limits on tree harvesting and reforestation requirements, charging mining and oil firms for the extraction of the raw resources that are owned by the state and implementation of carbon caps and trade systems.

In the final form of market failure – power imbalances of transacting players – regulation is expected to reduce the power imbalance and/or limit the behavior of the more powerful players. Antitrust legislation, for example, is aimed at directly addressing market structure failures. Price limits that "natural" monopolists such as railroads or telephone companies charge is another common example of legislation that has been put in place to limit the impact of market structure failures. Other examples include labor laws concerning minimum wage and health and safety standards; these laws are intended to protect workers that are seen to be in a weaker negotiating position and therefore unable to independently negotiate a fair labor contract. Examples of legislation aimed at limiting the informational, or influence, imbalance between transacting players include requirements for full disclosure on products such as food, cars, cigarettes and company stocks and limits on forms of advertising to children.

Four sources of regulatory and legislative failure and NGO accountability

The complaint ultimately giving rise to advocacy NGOs is that neither the legislative nor the regulatory system sufficiently addresses market failures. There are four sources of these perceived regulatory and legislative failures:

1. Identification and agreement that there is a market failure problem that needs to be addressed.
2. Different philosophical positions regarding the extent to which government should intervene in the market.
3. A power imbalance in the political system.
4. Undue influence of some stakeholders in the political process, and resource constraints in terms of money, expertise or span of control.

In looking at each of these sources, we will use the climate change issue in the context of the US regulatory and legislative system as an example to highlight these perceived failures.

Agreement that there is a market failure problem that needs to be addressed

The first potential source of legislative or regulatory shortcomings is that the legislators or regulators simply fall short of identifying an issue as a market failure that needs to be addressed. Some NGOs have complained that US legislators have failed to see climate change as a true and significant problem meriting governmental intervention. For example, some US politicians, such as Senator Inhofe, have argued that environmentalists and the media have played the "greatest hoax perpetrated on the American people" by supporting the idea that humans are responsible for global warming.

Different philosophical positions regarding the extent to which government should intervene in the market

The second potential source of legislative or regulative failure stems from a philosophical position concerning the appropriate limits of governmental intervention in the market. For example, again in the case of climate change, there can be agreement that climate change is a significant problem that needs to be addressed, but there is disagreement about where to place the responsibility; it is still under debate as to whether the market is best equipped to address the issue, or if legislation may be necessary. In fact, one of the key drivers of the rise of advocacy NGOs in the US and Europe in the 1990s was in response to some of the consequences of the laissez-faire approach of non-intervention that characterized the Reagan and Thatcher period.

A power imbalance in the political system

The third source of regulative or legislative failure is the undue influence of some players in the political process. Discussion of this source of regulative or legislative failure merits a brief summary of two theories of political economy. Political scientists and economists have tried to provide descriptive theories of how regulations are established. Early public interest theory, while supposedly descriptive, was closer to normative. Public interest theory argued that regulations are implemented primarily to maximize social welfare. This theory fell out of favor as it was shown that much regulation was not obviously maximizing social welfare and was often created to serve very specific interests at the expense of general welfare.[15]

Olsen, Stigler, Peltzman, Becker and others have, in response to this shortcoming, developed a private interest theory of regulation.[16] This theory holds that regulatory change is driven by competition among various special interest groups. In general, smaller, more cohesive groups with more to gain or lose tend to be most effective in overcoming freerider problems and implementing favorable regulations. Their effectiveness is also greater when those who will bear the costs of the regulations they are pursuing are widely diffused and the losses of individual parties are relatively small. Under these circumstances, these groups will be less able to build a strong counter-pressure group.

Interest groups that manage to overcome hurdles of collective action may attempt to pressure legislators and regulators through campaign contributions, votes or employment opportunities, thus effectively "capturing" these government officials. This then transforms into another source of regulative or legislative failure. A common complaint among NGOs pushing for increased legislation to address market failures is that well-organized and well-financed industry groups or individual firms are able to "capture" their regulators and legislators.

As a result, these regulators and legislators do not appropriately
address the market failures. Again, using the example of climate
change, the influence of some of the oil majors in the US, such as
ExxonMobil, on the regulatory and legislative position has been quite
significant. In fact, it was so intense it prompted a request to Exxon-
Mobil from Senators Rockefeller and Snowe to cease its influential
political activities denying global warming as a significant problem.[17]

As another example, NGOs have waged major campaigns against
the pharmaceutical industry concerning its perceived undue influence
in shaping the World Trade Organization's (WTO) TRIPS (trade-
related aspects of intellectual property rights) agreement surrounding
intellectual property (IP) protection for medicines. The complaint is
that the resulting IP legislation unduly favored the interests of the
pharmaceutical industry over broader social interests. Similar complaints have been waged against the US Department of the Interior as
being "captured" by the forestry and mining industries.

Undue influence of some stakeholders in the political process

The fourth and final source of regulative or legislative failure is
resource constraints in terms of money, expertise or span of control.
Even when governmental bodies have identified an issue as a market
failure requiring regulatory intervention and have significant political
freedom to make decisions, they may still fail to adequately address
the issues simply because of a lack of resources and influence. It has
been argued, for example, that regulatory bodies such as the US Food
and Drug Administration and the US Patent Office are not sufficiently
well-endowed in terms of resources and expertise to adequately meet
their regulatory responsibilities.

Furthermore, there are a number of problems that span across lines
of jurisdiction such as pollution, climate change, fisheries, disparities
in wealth across countries and so forth. Single governments, even
well-resourced ones with the political will to address the problems,
lack the span of control necessary to effectively deal with such issues.
Many of these problems are complicated by classic "tragedy of the
commons" dynamics in which joint coordination and sacrifice are
needed for the greater good, but in which every player has incentives
to leave the sacrifice for others.

In order to deal with the transnational problems involved in
globalization, governments have joined forces and created global

institutions to try to tackle these challenges. Trans-governmental (or supranational) organizations have been created, of which some have been growing in importance and power, especially those linked to international trade and finance, such as the WTO and the International Monetary Fund (IMF). Yet some of these trans-governmental organizations, such as the UN and the World Health Organization (WHO), are seen as lacking the authority or resources to address global problems. These global associations leave transnational problems unresolved, given the "cumbersome deliberations" that take place within them and, as Teegen *et al.* emphasize, "many global problems are simply too complex and pervasive for any one sector to handle alone."[18]

Other trans-governmental organizations, such as the WTO, the IMF and the World Bank, are seen as having the necessary authority and resources, but seem to fall short of addressing market failures adequately because of the other above-mentioned reasons for legislative or regulatory failure. For example, in the late 1990s many NGOs rose to fight against what they take to be the dominance of economic interests, and more specifically, developed countries' corporate interests in the WTO. The 1998 Seattle street demonstrations during the ministerial meeting of the WTO were, in fact, a defining moment in the creation of the anti- or alter-globalization movement.

Overall, there are situations in which both the market and the states are perceived as failing to meet society's needs. This context of perceived market and regulatory failure provide the raison d'être for advocacy NGOs. And clearly the greater the perceived extent and impact of these market and regulatory failures – whether the problems are in terms of creation and distribution of wealth, social and political justice or environmental concerns – the greater the perceived need for NGOs.

NGO accountability

Interestingly, if one refers back to Figure 2.1, with market failure being addressed by regulators and NGOs and regulatory failure being addressed only by NGOs, the obvious questions arise: What about NGO failure? Who are NGOs accountable to and what happens if they act "irresponsibly"? Many NGOs have much less accountability or transparency than many governmental bodies and publicly listed firms.

Both critics of NGOs as well as NGOs themselves are worried about this lack of accountability. Adversaries of some NGOs have launched initiatives to reign in and hold accountable increasingly influential NGOs. For example, the American Enterprise Institute, in cooperation with the Federalist Society for Law and Public Policy Studies, has presented a program initiative called "NGO Watch," which challenges the actions and statements of many NGOs.

Major NGOs have themselves struggled to develop some sort of system of self-regulation to ensure that the whole industry is not tarnished by the actions of a few irresponsible players. They recognize that as their influence grows so too will demands for greater professionalism, transparency and accountability. They also recognize that many NGOs are much more dependent on their good name than either governments or firms. Governments can rely on their power of sovereignty and firms can often still sell a product if they lose their good name as a company, or work to alter perceptions through subsidiaries. The ability of NGOs to attract critical resources of capital and labor depend almost entirely on their good names. As the role and power of NGOs continue to expand, the issue of accountability will become more relevant and substantial.

The rising influence of advocacy NGOs[19]

The perceived need for another set of organizations – beyond market players and governmental players – to address market and regulatory failure is apparent. NGOs can fill this gap by providing social benefits in terms of services and representation that neither the market nor the regulators provide.[20]

Yet, perceived market and regulatory failure are *not sufficient* to ensure that NGOs arise and become significant actors. The political, social, economic and technological environments all affect the ability of NGOs to develop and impact society. For example, Haiti, Uzbekistan, Somalia and North Korea all arguably have greater market and regulatory failure than the US or various European countries, but have nothing approaching the vibrancy of the civil society sector of these countries. Why not? In the remainder of this chapter, we will look at the political, economic, social and technological conditions that support or hamper the existence and influence of advocacy NGOs. We will not specifically and separately deal with the conditions necessary to support service NGOs, as these are, for the most part, a subset of the conditions necessary for the support of advocacy NGOs.

Political conditions

Changes in the political system of Western industrialized societies made them increasingly receptive and vulnerable to organized protest. Of particular importance are increasing social and political freedom, the emergence of the welfare state and the subsequent retreat of the state in matters of welfare.

For NGOs to arise, social and political freedom is a sine qua non condition: absence of repression or repressive social control, opportunity for open political dialogue, free association and freedom of speech are clearly elementary prerequisites for the organization of collective action in the form of advocacy NGOs. Interestingly, as democracy and free market-based economic systems have tended to emerge in parallel in Western societies, we have also seen the parallel development in the societal importance of corporations on the one hand, and NGOs on the other.

Economic conditions

Prosperity is a "pre-condition of social movement activity."[21] One of the greatest predictor variables of social movement activism is wealth. Organizing and agitating take resources, time and energy. If individuals are insufficiently wealthy to dedicate resources, time and energy to activism, then social activism becomes less likely. In some sense, then, activism is a "luxury good." This is further exemplified by the enormous increase in the number of NGOs in growing economies such as India and China. Also, as many NGOs rely on external funding to operate, sufficient resources must be available in their environment.

Social conditions

Intimately linked to this increase in wealth in Western industrialized societies are the accompanying shifts in societal trends and value systems. Social and political freedoms, added to economic liberalism, resulted in postindustrial capitalist economies and modernistic conceptions of society that drove the state to intervene in previously private areas of life. During the postwar phase, numerous countries were experimenting with various economic systems, including socialist systems in which capitalism in general, and the multinational enterprise in particular, were seen as a threat to societal wellbeing. As such, in parallel to increased capitalism, socialist ideals grew in importance from the nineteenth century on in order to satisfy public needs not addressed by the market economy, giving rise to the emergence and expansion of the welfare state. The state could not address all public needs not covered by the market, and as such, social movements "can be seen as efforts to regain control over decisions and areas of life increasingly subject to state control."[22]

Simultaneously, this prosperity results in an expansion of the intellectual classes. Mass higher education has resulted in the development of a whole new pool of individuals with more intellectual freedom and a greater exposure to information and ideas. In addition, the individuals of the intellectual classes often live concentrated in urban areas and students often live on or near university campuses. This geographic concentration facilitates organization, as exemplified by the student uprisings of the 1960s and 1970s,[23] and the level of prior organization provides the infrastructure supportive of emerging movements.[24] Furthermore, the majority of students involved in social and political movements are young, relatively free of familial demands and often more passionate than other age groups. This trend, coupled with growing uncertainty about future job prospects and security, makes this new class of young individuals potential recruits to social movements.

Finally, mass higher education has provided for a growing labor pool of skilled professional activists. Competencies among advocacy NGOs in organizing, lobbying and working with the media have all grown as a result. Activism has become, to some extent, a profession. "Central to the interplay of NGOs and globalization are the increasing numbers of knowledgeable and affluent individuals with time and resources to focus on promoting 'higher order' interests beyond mere subsistence."[25]

Technological conditions

The rise of information and telecommunication technologies has supported the growth in numbers and influence of NGOs in terms of organizing, collecting information around issues and ideas and distributing information. Creating an NGO depends on identifying individuals with shared interests. Internet sites dedicated to given issues bring together like-minded people who can then use the Internet to organize themselves faster, at lower costs and with less effort. The Internet also provides a vast set of resources for learning best practices around organizing and allows less experienced individuals and NGOs to learn from those with more experience.

Additionally, NGOs are often small and resource-poor and the Internet has also increased the ease with which NGOs can work together in coalitions around a specific issue. The use of coalitions is now the norm rather than the exception, with sites such as www. corpwatch.org, www.multinationalmonitor.org and www.indymedia. org serving as points of organization for many NGOs and individuals working on different issues. Finally, NGO street actions that might prompt clampdowns by authorities are often spontaneously organized via cell phone and text messaging.

Information and telecommunication technologies also help in terms of distributing information around given issues as well as sharing of ideas and ideologies. Peer-to-peer information sharing via email lists and blogs has created global dialogue around issues. Furthermore, information around a specific issue, for example the practices of Shell in Nigeria, can quickly be disseminated across the globe from a source on the ground in Nigeria.

NGOs are, ultimately, purveyors of information, ideas and ideology. Technology has increased their ability to allocate their wares, both through traditional distribution channels, such as newspapers, radio and television, and through more direct-to-consumer channels such as blogs and podcasts. The lower price and higher quality of technologies used to record digital content has allowed very small, low-budget NGOs to capture, package and distribute content to shape a debate anywhere in the world. A classic example of this is the group Witness. Witness, an NGO dedicated to exposing human rights abuses around the world, collects documentary video from individuals or groups and promotes and distributes the information via traditional as well as new media outlets.

Future trends

While we can only give cursory assessments at this point, several trends may be underway. First, one could look at the growth in wealth in the major developing countries such as Brazil, Russia, India and China. We can expect greater social demand in addressing market and regulatory failures in these countries. In more democratic countries such as India, this is already being reflected in the growth of advocacy NGOs. In China, we note that NGOs alternatively grow or shrink in response to the political climate in the country at any given time. We generally see a trend toward more political openness in China, but the trend is not constant and is subject to political reversal.

Second, with greater economic inequality both within and across countries, coupled with heightened information flows and the resulting awareness of disparities, we expect to see more dissatisfaction and agitation against this disproportional resource allocation in developing countries. This will likely play out in more NGOs that are interested in developing country issues campaigning for changes by both firms and regulators and legislators.

Third, we see something of a swing in the US and the UK toward a more nuanced version of laissez-faire capitalism. There seems to be greater discomfort and dissatisfaction with the market failures associated with globalization and a laissez-faire regulatory approach. With the diminishing reputation of the corporate sector in the wake of a multitude of scandals, a move to a more tightly regulated environment is expected.

Finally, we see a major and very interesting shift in the political landscape. In the 1990s we often saw conflicting political agendas between major business interests in the US and EU on the one side (pushing for less regulation and more free trade) and NGOs on the other (concerned with the negative consequences of globalization and de-regulation). Today we see early indications that these two interest groups are becoming more aligned. Specifically, US and EU corporations are increasingly realizing that the higher environmental and labor standards that they face in their countries are not going to go away and that these standards put them at a serious disadvantage relative to lower-cost, lower-standard countries. We expect that increasing numbers of US and EU companies are going to begin working with NGOs on supporting a basis of trade that supports higher global labor and environmental standards. Based on these trends that affect the underlying drivers of the growth of NGOs, we can expect that the number and influence of NGOs will continue to grow in many countries and in the global arena.

Conclusion

In this chapter we have detailed the types and sources of market and regulatory failure that leave societal needs unmet and thereby create a "demand" for the "products" of NGOs. We have also identified the necessary societal conditions for NGOs to be founded, grow and have an impact on society. By studying the fundamental drivers behind the recent explosive growth in the role of NGOs in many societies, we are in a better position to understand and predict where and under what conditions we are likely to see the role of NGOs shrink or grow.

Notes

1 R. V. Aguilera, D. E. Rupp, C. A. Williams and J. Ganapathi, "Putting the S back in corporate social responsibility: A multi-level theory of social change in organizations," *Academy of Management Review* 32 (3) (2007), 836–863.

2 J. P. Doh and H. J. Teegen (eds.), *Globalization and NGOs: Transforming Business, Government, and Society* (Westport: Praeger, 2003).

3 A. Kellow, "Norms, interests, and environment NGOs: the limits of cosmopolitanism," *Environmental Politics* 9 (3) (1999), 1–22.

4 Independent Sector, *The New Nonprofit Almanac and Desk Reference: The Essential Facts and Figures for Managers, Researchers, and Volunteers* (San Francisco: Jossey Bass, 2002).

5 United States Agency for International Development (USAID), *The Global Development Alliance: Public-private Alliances for Transformational Development* (Washington, DC: USAID Office of Global Development Alliances, 2006).

6 M. Yaziji, *Institutional Change and Social Risk: A Study of Campaigns by Social Movement Organizations against Firms* (Doctorial Dissertation, 2004).

7 World Bank, *Working with NGOs* (Washington, DC: The World Bank, 1995).

8 S. L. Hart and M. B. Milstein, "Creating sustainable value," *Academy of Management Executive* 17 (2) (2003), 58.

9 H. Teegen, J. P. Doh and S. Vachani, "The importance of nongovernmental organizations (NGOs) in global governance and value creation: An international business research agenda," *Journal of International Business Studies* 35 (6) (2004), 463–483.

10 Doh and Teegen (eds.), *Globalization and NGOs*.

11 J. P. Doh and T. Guay, "Corporate social responsibility, public policy and NGO activism in Europe and the United States: An institutional-stakeholder perspective," *Journal of Management Studies* 43 (1) (2006), 47–73.

12 M. Yaziji, "Toward a theory of social risk: Antecedents of normative delegitimation," *International Studies of Management and Organization* 34 (4) (2005), 87–107.

13 J. L. Campbell, "Why would corporations behave in socially responsible ways? An institutional theory of corporate social responsibility," *Academy of Management Review* 32 (3) (2007), 947–967.

14 A. Florini, *The Coming Democracy: New Rules for Running a New World* (Washington, DC: Island Press, 2003).

15 G. J. Stigler, *Chicago Studies in the Political Economy* (Chicago: Chicago University Press, 1988).

16 M. Olsen Jr., *The Logic of Collective Action: Public Goods and the Theory of Groups* (Cambridge, MA: Harvard University Press, 1965); G. J. Stigler, "The theory of economic regulation," *Bell Journal of Economics* 2 (1) (1971), 3–21; S. Peltzman, "Toward a more general theory of regulation," *Journal of Law & Economics* 19 (2) (1976), 211; G. S. Becker, "A theory of competition among pressure groups for political influence," *Quarterly Journal of Economics* 98 (3) (1983), 371.

17 A. C. Revkin, "Bush aide softened greenhouse gas links to global warming," *New York Times* June 8 (2005); Letter from Senators Rockefeller and Snowe to ExxonMobil CEO Rex Tillerson, Oct 30 (2006).

18 Teegen, Doh and Vachani, "The importance of nongovernmental organizations," 470.

19 Apart from where specified, significant proportions of this analysis are attributable to D. McAdam, J. D. McCarthy and M. N. Zald, "Social Movements," in N. Smelser (ed.), *Handbook of Sociology* (Newbury Park: Sage, 1988), pp. 695–737.

20 Teegen, Doh and Vachani, "The importance of nongovernmental organizations," 463–483.

21 N. J. Smelser (ed.), *Handbook of Sociology* (Newbury Park: Sage, 1988), p. 702.

22 Smelser (ed.), *Handbook of Sociology*, p. 701.

23 J. D'Emilio, *Sexual Politics, Sexual Communities* (Chicago: University of Chicago Press, 1983).

24 J. Freeman, "The origins of the women's liberation movement," *American Journal of Sociology* 78 (1973), 792–811; A. Morris, *The Origins of the Civil Rights Movement* (New York: Free Press, 1984).

25 Teegen, Doh and Vachani, "The importance of nongovernmental organizations," 471.

3 | *The emergence of NGOs in the context of ethical and institutional complexity*

What are the roles and responsibilities of the corporation? What should corporations do and not do? Where does the boundary lie between moral obligation and discretionary corporate action to improve societal wellbeing? As well as facing all the complexity involved in simply navigating toward a single goal of sustained profitable growth, firms are simultaneously being challenged about the appropriateness of such a singular goal. There are seemingly ever-increasing calls from various stakeholders such as NGOs, unions, financial markets and governments for businesses to take on additional social or economic goals beyond mere financial performance.

The evolution of complex responsibilities

At the very heart of this complexity is a single critical fact: firms increasingly operate under multiple, inexplicit, incomplete, often conflicting and continually re-negotiated social contracts and institutions. *Social contracts* can be defined as a real or hypothetical agreement expressing shared beliefs, norms and values concerning the rights and responsibilities of the state, non-state actors and citizens within a country. *Institutions* can be defined as highly resilient social and governance structures that express and enforce these beliefs, norms and values.[1] These institutions govern firms' structures and behaviors, provide resources and define what is appropriate and what is not. Firms that are better at meeting institutional demands will tend to have greater legitimacy and thereby have better access to resources and improve their chances of survival.[2]

The notion of a social contract dates back to Hobbes and Locke who envisioned a single implicit social contract between citizens and the sovereign. However, there are also implicit social contracts concerning the roles and responsibilities not only between the state and the citizenry, but also among various non-state actors and citizens. It is the multiplicity, inexplicitness, flux and disagreement across individuals, groups and countries about what constitutes appropriate and inappropriate firm behavior that underlies the institutional complexity facing firms today. Different individuals, groups and countries hold different beliefs about what is legitimate or illegitimate for a firm to do. For example, while Friedman famously said that the "business of business is business" others have held corporations to a wider range of social obligations.[3]

There is deep complexity along at least two different dimensions: ethical complexity and institutional complexity. In this chapter we will focus on how these two forms of complexity impact on the understanding and efforts of multinational corporations to pursue corporate social responsibility (CSR) and sustained profitable growth.[4]

From this point, we will first discuss the ethical complexity and its consequences for everyday decision-making and interpersonal dynamics in the workplace. We will then move on to discuss the institutional complexity and its consequences. As we shall see, ethical and institutional complexities are fundamentally related and tend to reinforce each other.

Ethical complexity

Ethical complexity is the result of difficulty in establishing clear ethical truths. As an academic field, ethics is filled with ambiguity and uncertainty. As a result, in many situations figuring out with certainty what constitutes the responsibility of the firm is, we will argue, impossible. Managers who are personally motivated to do the right thing can easily be overwhelmed with various ethical conundrums. Even the best professional ethicists will be the first to admit that they have no ready pat answers. In fact, those who do claim to have such answers often end up undermining ethical behavior: since managers cannot make use of the abstract principles these ethicists try to promote, they prefer to ignore the whole ethical question altogether.

Underlying dynamics
Any issue that has implications for people's welfare necessarily concerns norms and values. When norms and values are involved, there are no clear-cut guiding principles for the decision-maker, who is often torn between different values and ethical principles. As a result,

such issues frequently generate cognitive dissonance and emotional ambivalence for the person who is responsible for taking action.

Festinger's theory of cognitive dissonance specifies how individuals may hold inconsistent beliefs and how they attempt to resolve this dissonance.[5] While Festinger specified *cognitions* in his theory, individuals also experience *emotional ambivalence*, that is, "having mixed emotions and being torn in their attitude toward an object."[6]

Emotional ambivalence and cognitive dissonance become salient in contexts where moral judgment is required. Most people simultaneously hold multiple and conflicting moral beliefs and sentiments. We might, for example, feel or believe that killing an innocent being is always wrong, but simultaneously feel or believe that we may be morally obligated to kill innocents for the greater good or to prevent more killings of more innocents in the future. This ethical tension and conflict within a person is magnified by the inherent complexity of moral evaluations.

Moral reasoning – from specific moral claims about a particular action, down to the most foundational moral principles – is hierarchical, in that specific moral evaluations are built upon increasingly general and fundamental moral principles and values. We witness this whenever a justification for a specific moral claim is given. For instance, I might claim that it is morally appropriate to fib to a child about the existence of Santa Claus. Asked to defend this, I might say that it brings the child happiness, and that is why it is morally good. Pushed further, I might resort to a utilitarian argument that supports the claim that the right action is that which maximizes overall utility, and that fibbing, therefore, is morally appropriate in this context.

Moral philosophers have long recognized the distinction between different levels of moral thinking (moving from abstract to concrete, or, if you will, from fundamental to issue-specific). Scholars have made the distinction between narrow applications of moral principles and the general principles upon which they are based.[7] For example, *social contract theorists* have noted the difference between reasoning about what general social contract we are to adopt (e.g. *hypernorms*) and how to apply this contract in specific everyday situations (*micronorms*).[8] *Consequentialists* recognize the same distinctions between what defines the "good," how maximization of the good is to be calculated, and everyday moral evaluations using this maximizing principle.[9] *Rights theorists* recognize the distinction between rights (e.g. a negative right to life) and applications of the rights (e.g. what type of beings have this right). In the following analysis, we will focus on examples of how a single moral judgment is incredibly complex in terms of the number of levels at which there may be uncertainty.

Table 3.1 illustrates how different moral reasoning may look, depending on the level of abstraction and generality. The example is drawn from the human rights campaign claim which stated that workers at Nike's suppliers' factories in Vietnam were being mistreated.[10]

This table shows different levels of generality of reasoning and possible beliefs/sentiments and counter-beliefs/sentiments associated with it. These sets of beliefs, norms and values are "nested" in that some of them are more general and fundamental than others. If we start at the top of the chart, at Level 1, we find a belief that "respecting rights" is an inviolable moral principle. As suggested above, although many people in Western cultures agree that rights are sacred and inalienable, many of the same people also support the "counter-belief" that, for example, it is unfortunate, but morally acceptable, to unintentionally kill innocents in a justifiable war. There is some moral dissonance and ambivalence within individuals between beliefs/attitudes and counter-beliefs/attitudes at the same level of abstraction. One level down, even if one fully believes at Level 1 that respecting rights is an inviolable principle, one could be ambivalent about whether the application of this principle (Level 2) is enough to ensure that no rights are violated. At Level 3, the reasoning becomes more concrete, since it is applied to a specific societal context. However, the same phenomenon persists, in which a given belief and its counter-belief might coexist within an individual. Finally, when the fundamental principle is applied to a specific case (here, a Nike plant in Vietnam), the tension between mutually exclusive but coexisting beliefs remain. If we add up the issues and counter-issues of the various levels as we move through the table, we see how the complexities build upon one another. Complexity and dissonance at one level carry over to complexity and diverging opinions/beliefs at the next level. In this way, as we move down the table, the question of "What is the appropriate application or specification of the underlying principle?" becomes increasingly difficult to resolve with certainty.

Most individuals have dissonant beliefs and ambivalent feelings within different moral systems. Most of us draw on the various moral

Table 3.1. *Hierarchy of moral reasoning*

Level of generality	Issues of dissonance or ambivalence	Example of belief/sentiment	Example of counter-belief/sentiment
1. Basic principles	Foundational moral principles (e.g. rights-based, consequentialist, social contract, virtue theories).	Respecting rights is an inviolable moral principle.	Respecting rights is not an inviolable moral principle. Rights may be violated if doing so substantially increases overall social welfare and/or minimizes future rights violations.
2. Application of the basic principle	Theories of free choice; economic theories; definitions of "free market" and "mutual consent."	Free market arrangements are a form of mutual consent. As such, agreements made in the free market do not constitute violations of rights.	Free market arrangements are not a form of mutual consent because the differences in market power make free consent illusory.
3. General facts about the context	Facts about standard Vietnamese employer–employee relationships; categorization criteria of free market arrangements.	Standard Vietnamese employer–employee relationships are free market arrangements.	Standard Vietnamese employer–employee relationships are not free market arrangements because the government prevents unionization and distorts bargaining power.
4. Specific facts of the case	Facts about the firms; categorization criteria of standard Vietnamese employer–employee relationships.	Nike suppliers use standard Vietnamese employer–employee relationships.	Nike suppliers do not use standard Vietnamese employer–employee relationships.

systems that constitute our cultural heritage, and, as we have seen, things get even more complicated when we attempt to apply general principles to concrete situations. Importantly, various stakeholders, and particularly social movement organizations such as NGOs, typically leverage this moral ambiguity or conflict within the audience of critical players to delegitimize a particular organization or undermine a particular institution. (This is explained in depth in Chapter 4.) They often do this by first picking an extremely morally egregious action and then assigning responsibility for it to the targeted organization or institution. This tactic serves to intensify feelings of uncertainty in managers and employees and impede action.

Consequences

This great moral complexity has consequences for the individual manager, as well as for the relationship between various actors in the organization and their performance. First, for the individual, the cognitive dissonance, emotional ambivalence and uncertainty resulting from ethical dilemmas can slow down or entirely prevent decision-making.

Second, once a decision is made, these psychological states can quickly and powerfully dissipate the energy, commitment and effort toward a given course of action, since the individual will be constantly dogged by lingering doubts about the appropriateness of the action.

Third, conflicting ethical considerations, if played upon, can lead to inconsistency and misalignment across actions. Just as one cannot switch strategies too frequently for risk of dissipating momentum and failing to build on prior gains, decisions that are inconsistent as a result of following first one ethical principle then another can lead to poor performance.

Fourth, the complexity might lead to a refusal to accept responsibility for ethical deliberation and decision-making. When a manager faces too many conflicting opinions in his or her mind, he or she will tend to dismiss the morality of the subject altogether and replace the moral evaluation with some other standard or criterion of judgment. Typically, this means referring to a principle of profit maximization, or industry best practice, or the effect the decision will have on one's performance evaluation, or a combination of these. In the example outlined above, instead of trying to figure out the morally correct thing to do regarding Vietnamese factory workers, the manager might rather refer to what other companies in the region are doing or to what is best for the bottom line.

On a more interpersonal level, when a leader is perceived over time to be morally inconsistent or to lack integrity (which can be the perceived result of the ethical complexity and conflict within the leader), his or her influence over followers is threatened, and this can have disastrous effects on productivity.[11] Similarly, in teams, lack of alignment or agreement on what principles and values are going to be the basis for collaboration will have consequences for the performance of the team. In effect, the importance of value congruence in organizations is beyond doubt, and when latent moral conflicts persist, this will have clear negative effects on the organization's long-term performance.[12]

Institutional complexity

In addition to the moral ambiguity, the institutional context adds additional complexity to the picture. Corporations – especially multinational corporations – have resource dependencies on a large number of stakeholders whose different ideological and ethical perspectives are often competing or conflicting. These stakeholders can question whether a firm is living up to its responsibilities or whether it is acting legitimately. Powerful stakeholders that question the legitimacy of the firm or its actions can generate "social risk" for the firm, as we shall see in more detail below. Managers who are simply attempting to keep the firm profitable will find challenges in navigating this institutional complexity and the incompatible demands that it generates.

Companies exist in increasingly complex environments due to the ever-more globalized nature of their operations and markets. In these environments, various stakeholders often have conflicting demands in terms of what they expect of a company. In other words, their ideas of what constitutes the social responsibility of a given firm might vary to a great extent. How is an individual manager to deal with these conflicting demands? And, given the high and growing relevance of various stakeholders to firm performance, how can their demands be balanced to develop a coherent strategy that is both ethical and effective?

Underlying dynamics

Current societal realities, particularly globalization, are making it easier for stakeholders to more effectively voice their demands:

1. The vast anti-globalization movement is increasingly powerful and has developed strategies and tools that can seriously hurt corporations.[13]
2. Information flows ever-more freely, thanks to the media and the Internet. This in turn leads to better coordination between aligned interests and ideologies, as well as the possibility for anyone interested to observe and evaluate firms' actions.
3. The spread of democracy has set the context for stakeholders to more effectively voice their demands, and increasing awareness following democratization in Third World countries has led to an increase in the number and power of stakeholders.

It is important to note that, although conflicting *interests* are a serious risk to the company (as we shall see in more detail below), the diverging *ideologies* of the different stakeholders are even more important for the issue developed here. When we speak of ideology, we are in the domain of norms and values, and automatically depart from the domain of certainty, objectivity, predictability and the like. For a company, this has implications similar to those derived from moral ambiguity. So, as though the complexity due to diverging institutional demands were not enough, institutions are in addition suffused with value systems. In effect, core to institutions are the sets of beliefs, norms and values that characterize them.

Figure 3.1 illustrates the complexity managers face in terms of multiple, often conflicting, stakeholder demands. Stakeholders like NGOs, consumers, government agencies, international organizations and unions, by their nature, have diverging opinions on what a corporation should be doing for society. These opinions relate to the interests of the various stakeholders, as well as to more fundamental beliefs regarding what the role of business in society *should* be (i.e. its *normative* role). However, before looking more closely at this institutional and normative complexity, we first need to understand the notion of *legitimacy* of the firm.

Legitimacy

When a company does not live up to its stakeholders' expectations of what is morally right, its legitimacy is challenged. Legitimacy is the

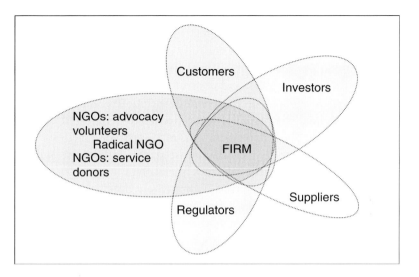

Figure 3.1 The context of the firm and its stakeholders

quality or state of being perceived or understood to be in accordance with a set of norms or values concerning what is desirable, proper or appropriate.[14] Legitimacy lies in the domain of social values and is indicative of the degree to which a firm complies with its society's moral evaluation of what the norms and values, means and ends of an organization should be.[15]

Legitimacy has some distinctive attributes that affect the way managers must deal with the dilemmas arising out of challenges to their firm. Legitimacy is a resource but is not "owned" in the same way as most other resources. It has a special attribute of *external control* that distinguishes it from most material resources. Ownership of property usually "consists of a bundle of rights which the owner of the property possesses with regard to some thing – rights to possess, use, dispose of, exclude others, and manage and control."[16] Given that legitimacy is essentially granted and revoked by individuals, organizations and institutions beyond the focal organization, organizations do not have this "bundle of rights" over their legitimacy as they do over their physical and some of their intellectual property. Firms do not own or fully control their own legitimacy; it is granted and revoked by those who evaluate the firm. The most difficult type of legitimacy to manage is normative legitimacy: is the firm acting in a way that corresponds to the value-based expectations of its stakeholders?

While normative legitimacy is not fully controlled by the focal firm, it is also not usually fully controlled by any single outside individual or organization. The sources and control of a focal firm's normative legitimacy are *distributed* or *fragmented*. Normative legitimacy is a socially constructed, perpetually negotiated status conferred upon a focal organization and dependent on many players' actions and evaluations. Some outside organizations, particularly those with a great deal of legitimacy and influence themselves, can affect others' judgment of a focal firm's legitimacy, but rarely do all the evaluators in the firm's environment judge it uniformly. Thus, normative legitimacy is inherently complex in nature, since different players have different opinions on what is the appropriate response of a company to a given social issue. These complex, distributed and often conflicting evaluations of the legitimacy of the firm are a great source of uncertainty for managers.

Consequences

In the past, strategy scholars have generally focused on four external risks – competitive, macroeconomic, technological and political. Of these, political risk is closest to social risk in the strategy literature; both literature streams center on firms' interactions with particular nonmarket players that can affect firm behavior and performance. Yet, fundamental differences between social risk and political risk indicate that social risk is sufficiently unique to require and merit attention from managers.

We can distinguish political risk from social risk in terms of actors, interaction dynamics, firm strategic behavior and consequences. First, apart from the firm, the primary actors in political risk are governments. These actors are clearly identifiable, relatively stable and occupy distinct and mostly non-overlapping domains. By contrast, the primary actors in social risk, such as NGOs, may not be readily identifiable, may arise and vanish relatively quickly, and may geographically overlap.

Second, the interactions between actors (evaluators, critical players and focal firms) are fundamentally different in political risk and social risk. Governments primarily govern only what firms do within their borders, while social pressure groups challenge actions carried out in other countries. The demands of governments are relatively clear, unitary and coherent, while those of various NGOs may be unclear, fragmented and contradictory. Governments have sovereign powers to impose their will; NGOs do not and have only indirect influence on firms via third parties (e.g. consumers, government, media).

Third, the strategic options of firms facing political and social risk are quite distinct. Strategies such as avoidance, defiance or manipulation may be more feasible with NGOs, which have relatively less direct coercive power, than with governments. Finally, the consequences of political risk center on government actions including regulation, taxation and nationalization. Social risk can lead to political risk – and thus have these consequences – but it also includes a market-size effect. Examples of this include what we have seen in areas such as hydroelectric dams, nuclear energy, furs and tobacco in the United States and much of Western Europe over the last twenty years,[17] a firm's market share, reputation and so forth.

These fundamental differences between social risk and political risk emphasize the strategic importance of firms paying heed to the role of legitimacy and its relevance to decision-making. In sum, the consequences of institutional complexity and social risk must not be underestimated. If a firm stays exclusively focused on abiding by the law and complying with regulations (i.e. ensuring *political legitimacy*), it does not mean that it has avoided all risk to the company's reputation and performance.

Conclusion

In this chapter we have used a neo-institutional framework as a basis for understanding the institutional environment as a whole. We have attempted to provide a finer-grained analysis of the normative institutional complexity surrounding firms at the inter-organizational level as well as at the inter- and intra-personal levels.

As multinationals come under increasing scrutiny and ethical evaluation, they face an explosion in the degree of complexity in their world. The familiar complexity of simply running a multinational profitably is crossed with the complex and ambiguous realm of ethics and legal systems, which in turn is crossed with a broader range of increasingly vocal stakeholders expressing a range of institutional ideologies as well as interest groups. It is by no means an easy feat to overcome divergent needs ranging from institutional priorities to societal values, and in many instances, managers will defer to a simpler evaluative system when overloaded with options. Despite this tendency, it is still more advantageous to the firm and society at large to have a variety of choices which will ultimately serve at least one relevant objective.

Notes

1 R. W. Scott, *Institutions and Organizations* (Thousand Oaks: Sage, 2001).
2 For more on neo-institutional theory, see W. W. Powell and P. J. DiMaggio (eds.), *The New Institutionalism in Organizational Analysis* (Chicago: University of Chicago Press, 1991). For a deeper discussion of the three pillars of institutional theory see Scott, *Institutions and Organizations*.
3 See, for example, J. Freeman, "The origins of the women's liberation movement," *American Journal of Sociology* 78 (1973), 79–811.
4 For a comprehensive review of the "strategic" use of corporate social responsibility, see D. Vogel, *The Market for Virtue: The Potential and Limits of Corporate Social Responsibility* (Washington, DC: Brookings Institution Press, 2005).
5 L. Festinger, *A Theory of Cognitive Dissonance* (Stanford: Stanford University Press, 1957).
6 D. W. Jamieson, "The attitude ambivalence construct: Validity, utility, measurement," Paper presented at the American Psychological Association, Toronto (1993); J. R. Priester and R. E. Petty, "The gradual threshold models of ambivalence: Relating the positive and negative bases of attitudes to subjective ambivalence," *Journal of Personality and Social Psychology* 71 (3) (1996), 431–449; J. R. Priester and R. E. Petty, "Extending the bases of subjective attitudinal ambivalence: Interpersonal and intrapersonal antecedents of evaluative tension," *Journal of Personality and Social Psychology* 80 (1) (2001), 19–34.
7 T. Donaldson and T. W. Dunfee, "Towards a unified conception of business ethics: Integrative social contracts theory," *Academy of Management Review* 19 (2) (1994), 252–284.
8 See Donaldson and Dunfee, "Towards a unified conception"; T. Hobbes, *Leviathan* (Oxford: Oxford University Press, 1996); R. Nozick, *Anarchy, State and Utopia* (Oxford: Blackwell, 1977); J. Rawls, *A Theory of Justice* (Cambridge, MA: Harvard University Press, 1971); J. Rawls, *Political Liberalism* (New York: Columbia University Press, 1993).

9 R. Hare, *Moral Thinking: Its Levels, Method and Point* (Oxford: Oxford University Press, 1981); J. S. Mill, *Utilitarianism* (London: Oxford University Press, 1863/1988).

10 The table is a single, illustrative representation of sources of internal dissonance and ambivalence in our moral belief systems. It is intended to be illustrative and not an exhaustive or exclusive representation of such ambiguity and contradiction. There are multiple plausible ways of dividing up the levels, and multiple ways of framing the issues.

11 For recent evidence in leadership research, see J. Antonakis, A. T. Cianciolo and R. Sternberg (eds.), *The Nature of Leadership* (Thousand Oaks: Sage, 2004); B. Bass, *Transformational Leadership: Industry, Military, and Educational Impact* (Mahwah: Lawrence Erlbaum Associates, 1998).

12 J. Chatman, "Matching people and organizations: Selection and socialization in public accounting firms," *Administrative Science Quarterly* 39 (4) (1991), 459–484.

13 M. Yaziji, "Turning gadflies into allies," *Harvard Business Review* February (2004), 110–115.

14 M. C. Suchman, "Managing legitimacy: Strategic and institutional approaches," *Academy of Management Review* 20 (3) (1995), 571–610.

15 P. Selznick, *Leadership in Administration* (Berkeley: University of California Press, 1957).

16 D. Votaw, *Modern Corporations* (Englewood Cliffs: Prentice-Hall, 1965), pp. 96–97.

17 For example, according the World Commission on Dams, *Dams and Development* (London: Earthscan Publishers, 2000), dam commissions in North America dropped 90 percent from the 1960s to the 1990s, primarily because of various stakeholder concerns. Similarly, per capita cigarette consumption in the US has dropped by more than 50 percent (from 4,345 cigarettes per person in 1963 to 2,025 in 2000) according to the US Department of Agriculture's "Tobacco: Situation and Outlook," various issues.

Case illustration: genetically modified organisms, social movements and NGOs

The agricultural biotech (AgBiotech) industry – producing genetically engineered crop seeds – is young, having only become commercially significant in 1996. At that point, companies such as Monsanto, Aventis, Syngenta (created through a merger of the agricultural activities of Novartis and AstraZeneca), BASF and Dupont were becoming the primary producers of genetically engineered seeds. These seeds would soon be available worldwide and come in various forms. Herbicide tolerant plants, accounting for approximately 73 percent of global genetically engineered crop area, simply have structures that make crops more resistant to pesticides used commercially to control infestation. Insect resistant plants, accounting for approximately 22 percent of global genetically engineered crop area, are manufactured to produce pesticides within the plant as another way to deter infestation.[1] "Stacked" plants are both herbicide tolerant and insect resistant. Other genetically engineered seeds include virus-resistant strains and added-nutrient crops, in which increased levels of vitamins or minerals can be measured. These product offerings aided in catapulting the industry from virtually nothing in 1995 to a $2.7 billion industry in 1999, and more than $4.75 billion in 2002.[2] During this phase, analysts were singing the praises and the potential of the new industry. Companies in the industry and in the new broader "life sciences" category, which included pharmaceuticals, were rewarded with high multiples in their stock prices.

But starting in the mid-1990s, NGOs in Europe began a concerted and successful campaign against GMOs. Concerns ranging from sustainable development, consumer protection, farmer welfare, ethical concerns over genetic engineering, and the idea that the insect resistant plants would harm beneficial insects and soil organisms and lead to the development of new or worse viruses, piqued the interest of various NGOs. A broad coalition consisting of Greenpeace, Friends of the Earth (FoE), the Rural Advancement Foundation International

(RAFI), and a more general network of women's organizations, environmental groups, consumer associations and youth associations came together in an attempt to halt the widespread distribution of genetically engineered seeds. Various campaigns on the issue were pursued. There was the "Pure Food Campaign" and the "Global Days of Action Against Gene-Foods" in 1997 and 1998. In 1998, Physicians and Scientists Against Genetically Engineered Foods demanded a moratorium on the release of GMOs and GMO products in foods.[3] During this time, GMOs were increasingly being referred to as "Frankenfoods" and five countries in Europe decided they would not advocate GM crops, which the EU fully supported.[4] In April 1999, environmentalists became even more concerned when an entomologist at Cornell found that monarch butterfly larvae fed a diet of certain genetically engineered corn died in unusual numbers. In September 1999, activists from thirty countries filed a lawsuit against major AgBiotech companies asking for billions in damages for monopolistic practices. By the end of 1999, genetically modified crops were virtually nonexistent in Europe.[5] But the largest market for genetically modified seeds and crops had always been in the US. It appeared that the AgBiotech industry could weather the (temporary) negative attitudes toward GMO seeds and products in Europe.

Debates continued as analysts attempted to determine whether lower non-genetically engineered (GE) crop yield was due to higher market prices for non-GE crops, or if GE crops did in fact have value-added attributes. These soon came to a halt when French company Aventis Agriculture's StarLink corn was under scrutiny from the general public. The Environmental Protection Agency had given Aventis permission to grow StarLink corn for livestock feed or other non-food uses, but did not approve it for human consumption due to lingering concerns as to whether the corn would produce allergic reactions. The agreement was that a 660-foot buffer strip area had to be constructed between StarLink corn crops and any other food-destined crops, and that no StarLink product was to enter international commerce. In all, StarLink corn had been planted on less than 0.5 percent of total US corn acreage.

On September 17, 2000, Friends of the Earth, spearheaded by activist Larry Bohlen, together with other members of the Genetically Engineered Food Alert – a coalition of NGOs – publicized the results of DNA tests on Taco Bell taco shells in the US.[6] The story ran on CBS, CNN, ABC and Fox television stations as well as all major US newspapers on September 18. The test showed evidence of the presence of Aventis's StarLink corn that is toxic to European corn borers and certain other insect pests. Another 110,000 tests were performed, showing that more than 10 percent of all corn grain had traces of the genetically modified strain, indicating extensive commingling of corn products. Fanned by environmental and consumer advocacy NGOs, the crisis spiraled ever deeper. Soon Kraft, Safeway, Westin Family, Mission Foods, ConAgra Foods, Kellogg's and others were recalling products and shutting down plants. The costs to Aventis are expected to be $500 million, despite its quick response to criticisms. Less than ten days after the negative publicity, Aventis suspended sale of its seeds and recalled seeds that were a part of the 2000 growing season. The crisis cost executives in its Crop Sciences division their jobs and likely informed Aventis's decision to divest itself of the AgBiotech Crop Sciences division.

More critically for the AgBiotech industry as a whole, the StarLink affair threatened to turn public opinion in the US against genetically engineered seeds and crops. Public concern about health effects were heightened as it was publicized that forty-four people claimed illness was caused by Aventis corn. By mid-year 2001, "life science" companies were divesting themselves of their AgBiotech holdings and some analysts were claiming that the StarLink debacle, together with continuing successful NGO efforts to shape public opinion and public policy in the EU and the US against GMOs, pointed to a potentially moribund AgBiotech industry. The rapidity of the birth, rise and (threatened) decline of an industry is likely unparalleled.

Notes

1 "Speed bump or blow-out for GM seeds?," *Rural Advancement Foundation International* December 21 (2000), available at www.gene.ch/genet/2001/Jan/msg00000.html.
2 Elizabeth Becker, "US contests Europe's ban on some food," *New York Times* May 13 (2003), B4.
3 The European Commission, "Economic impacts of genetically modified crops on the agri-food sector," available at http://ec.europa.eu/agriculture/publi/gmo/fullrep/ch4.htm.
4 Scott Miller, "EU's new rules will shake up market for bioengineered food," *The Wall Street Journal* April 16 (2004), A1.

5 Andrew Hund, "Monsanto: Visionary or architect of bioserfdom? A global socio-economic examination of genetically modified organisms," December 10 (1999), available at www.mindfully.org/GE/Monsanto-Bioserfdom-Andrew-Hund.htm.

6 Jerry Perkins, "Iowa StarLink costs $9.2 million – Aventis CropScience pays claims to farmers, elevators," *Des Moines Register* September 15 (2001).

Case illustration: protecting the people – environmental NGOs and TXU Energy

The coal industry has been under intense regulatory and environmental pressures throughout the 1990s and especially in the early 2000s. During 2006, coal mining was listed as the fifth most dangerous profession in the US due to rising on-the-job fatalities, leading to a federal Miner Act to promote better safety measures.[1] Aside from immediate safety issues, the coal industry is also confronted with increased attention to global warming. Only four years ago, it was expected that shifting prices in natural gas would lead to a greater reliance on coal energy and coal-burning units. However, as global movements, such as the Kyoto Protocol, have gained attention, it is quite possible for worldwide global-warming regulations to gain a foothold. This has deterred companies from burning coal, since it releases such high levels of carbon dioxide that directly contributes to global warming, and had become the point of concern with TXU Corporation.[2]

In response to a predicted coal boom, TXU announced plans to build eleven new coal-burning power plants throughout Texas. Coal was abundant and inexpensive, and TXU saw an opportunity to capitalize on this before the US joined the ranks of other developed countries that have set greenhouse gas emission caps. It had been estimated that coal prices could increase six-fold, subsequently raising coal-powered electricity production by 50 percent.[3] Americans would not be ready for such a substantial increase, which posed a potential decade for TXU to provide inexpensive energy.

These plans almost immediately spurred mixed reactions. Analysts predicted an increase in TXU stock prices from calculated returns, while environmentalists and NGOs attempted to curb future construction of coal-burning power plants. In turn, one of the most interesting cases of corporate–NGO engagement in recent years occurred: the agreement reached among Kohlberg Kravis Roberts & Co. (KKR), Texas Pacific Group and several environmental NGOs, as part of KKR's acquisition of TXU, the electricity generator. After discussions with Environmental Defense and the Natural Resource Defense Council (NRDC), KKR and Texas Pacific Group agreed to scrap controversial plans by TXU to build eight new coal-fired power plants in Texas as part of a proposed buyout of Dallas-based electricity generator TXU Corporation.[4] Revising its plans for new power stations, the company will commit itself to cut carbon-dioxide emissions back to 1990 levels by 2020 and adopt strict environmental rules.

If the deal goes ahead it will be the biggest such leveraged buyout – a corporate acquisition financed with loans – in the history of the US. The team that set it up sought the help of some of the same environmental groups that had previously sued TXU over the company's environmental policies and aggressive expansion plans. "This is a watershed moment in America's fight against global warming," said Fred Krupp, president of Environmental Defense, a New York-based environmental group involved in the negotiations.[5] William K. Reilly, the former administrator for the Environmental Protection Agency under President George H. W. Bush, who now works for Texas Pacific, made the call to Mr. Krupp because he was one of the few environmentalists he trusted to keep the talks confidential and to work in a constructive manner.[6]

Details of this deal were announced on February 26, 2007. The private-equity firms and their banks, including Morgan Stanley and Goldman Sachs, agreed to pay $32 billion for TXU's stock and to assume more than $12 billion of the company's debts. The environmental aspects of the agreement seem likely to make the deal more acceptable to a wide range of interests. Under the new ownership the company says it will abandon plans for all but three of eleven coal-fired power plants. The three remaining plants will not be equipped with low-emissions technology, but will be designed in such a way that they could be fitted for carbon capture and storage in the future. In addition, the company has announced plans to invest $400 million in increasing the efficiency with which energy is used. It will also reduce emissions from existing plants and lobby for a cap-and-trade emissions scheme, which would provide it with carbon-emission permits that it could sell if it cuts its current emissions with more efficient plants.[7]

TXU also says that it will offer rebates on solar-panel investments by customers and continue to be the largest purchaser of wind-generated power in Texas, increasing its purchase to 1,500 megawatts. Texas governor Rick Perry announced in 2007 a public–private initiative to invest $10 billion in increasing Texas's wind power.[8] "It's a huge turnaround," says Dave Hawkins, director of NRDC's climate center. "A company that was until last week opposed to fighting global warming has now pledged to support mandatory carbon caps. The effort by the buyers does signal a change in the way carbon America thinks about climate change."

TXU's plans for the eleven new coal-fired power plants, announced in 2006, caused a storm of protest by politicians, religious groups and small-business owners when announced. In part as a result of this, the company's plans had already run into difficulty with the Texas legislature.

In an interesting twist in the case, Environmental Defense announced it had hired Perella Weinberg Partners, the boutique investment bank, to advise it as the group takes on an unusual role in the middle of the buyout. By reaching out to Perella Weinberg, Environmental Defense appears to be signaling that it wants an even more powerful seat at the bargaining table with TXU and its suitors. The move may presage a heightened role for environmental activists in mergers and acquisitions as they use Wall Street tactics and a better understanding of the financial mechanics of deals to negotiate even more aggressive environmental concessions.[9]

Mr. Krupp said that he had decided to hire the bankers because "we've never been involved in a buyout, and we wanted to make certain that we had the best expertise available." He played down the prospect that his organization, which years ago was thought to be business-friendly when that approach was spurned by other large environmental groups, might become active in seeking concessions in future energy deals.

"I don't know what the future's going to bring, but we are not attempting to parlay this into anything beyond making a real contribution" as the TXU purchase proceeds, he said.[10]

Notes

1 M. Dalton, "Expanding the mined," *Wall Street Journal* November 12 (2007), R8

2 Dalton, "Expanding the mined," R8.

3 J. Carey, "Coal: Could be the end of the line," *BusinessWeek* November 13 (2006), 74.

4 E. Souder, "TXU bidders would cut 8 of 11 proposed plants," *Dallas Morning News* February 25 (2007), A1.

5 Souder, "TXU bidders," A1.

6 A. R. Sorkin and F. Barringer, "Environmental group behind the TXU deal hires a banker," *New York Times* March 8 (2007), C1.

7 Souder, "TXU bidders," A1.

8 Sorkin and Barringer, "Environmental group," C1.

9 Sorkin and Barringer, "Environmental group," C1.

10 Sorkin and Barringer, "Environmental group," C1.

PART II

NGO *advocacy campaigns*

4 | NGO *campaigns against corporations and (de-)legitimacy*

NGO campaigns can severely threaten profitable firms and constrain their scope for strategic action. For example, under pressure by a coalition of advocacy NGOs, Aventis paid more than $500 million to buy back genetically modified StarLink corn from growers, fired the head of its US crop sciences division and spun off its agricultural business (see Case illustration on p. 46). In another case, the Free Burma Coalition of NGOs forced companies such as Levi Strauss, Macy's, Liz Claiborne, PepsiCo, Texaco, Amaco, ABN AMRO, Kodak, Apple, Disney, Motorola and many others out of Burma. Pharmaceutical companies have also been targeted as AIDS activist NGOs pressured them with threats of negative public relations regarding patents on AIDS drugs in South Africa. Companies targeted in that campaign included GlaxoSmithKline, Merck & Co., Bristol-Myers Squibb, Roche and others.

Peter Drucker stated that, "in the next society, the biggest challenge for the large company – especially for the multinational – may be its social legitimacy."[1] Raymond Vernon noted that these advocacy organizations were increasingly pushing firms, under threat of delegitimation and its attendant costs, in order to support the norms and values that the NGOs were dedicated to promote.[2] In this chapter we will start by highlighting how these campaigns represent an under-studied area of risk for firms. We will then turn to looking at the process and risk factors of these campaigns.

Social and political risk

Interestingly, given the high and growing relevance of the issue to firm performance, strategy scholars have generally failed to address the risk that these delegitimation campaigns raise for firms. To date, four types of external risks have primarily occupied strategy scholars: (1) competitive risk (concerning the future moves of suppliers, rivals, substitute producers, potential entrants and customers), (2) macro-economic risks (e.g., exchange rate shifts), (3) technological risks (e.g., unforeseen inventions and innovations); and (4) political risks (e.g., governmental policy changes such as asset seizure, taxation and regulation). Of these, social risk's closest phenomenal cousin from the Strategy literature is political risk; both literature streams center on firm interactions with particular nonmarket players who can affect firm behavior and performance. Yet, as noted above, fundamental differences between social risk and political risk indicate that social risk is sufficiently unique to require and merit a distinct line of research. However, as also noted in Chapter 3, social risk can aggravate political risk, as illustrated, in part, by the dynamics of NGO campaigns.

A neo-institutional understanding of campaigns

As we discussed in Chapter 3, NGO campaigns may be viewed from the perspective of strategic management. However, a neo-institutional framing may give the greatest insight into the dynamics and antecedents of these campaigns. We discuss these campaigns as a form of *normative delegitimation* – the process by which an organization's normative legitimacy is diminished through challenges by outside organizations. While this description allows for the possibility that organizations other than NGOs may be engaged in delegitimation campaigns, in practice, NGOs are the primary organizations behind these campaigns and the study here will be limited to this context. This description builds on existing definitions. In particular, we use Suchman's definition of *legitimacy* as the quality or state of being perceived or understood to be in accordance with a set of norms or values concerning what is desirable, proper or appropriate.[3] We also use Scott's analytic distinction of *normative legitimacy* (as opposed to cultural–cognitive or regulative forms of legitimacy) as a form of legitimacy that lies in the domain of social values[4] and is indicative of the degree of society's moral evaluation of the norms and values, means and ends of an organization.[5]

Neo-institutional theory scholars have developed a robust general theoretical framework that lends support to many of the ideas and relationships among the concepts central to delegitimation campaigns. Significant research has been conducted concerning how organizations attempt to create, maintain and restore legitimacy,[6] particularly in the face of competing institutional demands.[7] A great deal of early institutional theory literature has also tested and confirmed hypotheses tying organizational legitimacy to organizational performance and survival.[8] However, relatively little research has been done on the antecedents and inter-organizational processes of organizational delegitimation campaigns.

This chapter is primarily interested in addressing two main questions: (1) What are the basic dynamics of these campaigns? And (2) under what conditions is a firm at most risk for being attacked in a delegitimation campaign? Specifically with respect to the second question, we identify the firm attributes, institutional context and broader social factors that increase a firm's risk for being the target of a delegitimation campaign.

In addition to addressing these questions of significance to both strategy and organizational theory scholars, there is a deeper theoretical impetus behind this chapter. Specifically, the chapter is intended to bring greater agency and strategic considerations into our accounts of institutional pressure and institutional change. While there is rich literature on strategic organizational *responses* to institutional pressure, with Oliver's typology of generic strategies providing a powerful framework, there is considerably less research into the strategic agency of the organizations responsible for the institutional pressure.[9] The advocacy organizations that carry out these campaigns are institutionally proactive agents in that they either hold firms accountable to institutional norms, or, quite differently, they pursue institutional change through their campaigns against firms. A full understanding of institutional pressure, then, requires insight into the goals, strategies and tactics of the organizations applying the pressure.

The process of normative delegitimation

A model of the social-risk process is provided in Figure 4.1. It is worth emphasizing that this model sacrifices accuracy for simplicity and generality[10] as is appropriate for an introductory and orienting model.

The social-risk process begins with a multilevel set of antecedents including firm, institutional and social movement factors. These antecedents lead to evaluations and possibly delegitimation attempts – what we call challenges by NGOs – which can take manifold forms including boycotts, brand bashing, lobbying, lawsuits and activist–shareholder resolutions.

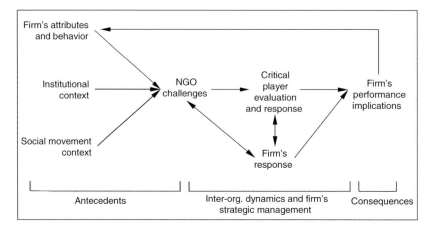

Figure 4.1 Social risk process

NGOs are the primary vectors of normative delegitimation. Examples of NGOs include groups such as WWF, Greenpeace, Friends of the Earth, Adbusters, Foundation for a Smokefree America, People for the Ethical Treatment of Animals (PETA), Human Rights Watch, Common Cause and Public Citizen.[11]

NGOs' influence over firms is indirect because they are non-governmental and hence cannot directly institute laws or regulations to thereby coerce firms. NGOs also lack the direct financial leverage over firms that suppliers, customers and rivals have. Thus they have, in Frooman's typology, a low interdependence relationship with low stakeholder power.[12]

Consequently, NGOs use indirect pressure[13] to influence firm behavior via *critical players* – organizations that do have direct influence over the firm's behavior, economic performance, or both. These include regulators, the courts, politicians, voters, consumers, employees, suppliers, shareholders and others who have some influence over the firm's economic outcomes. Their power can take the form of regulations and fines, court decisions, taxation, laws, purchase decisions, refusal to do business, and shareholder resolutions directing and restraining management choices. It is worth noting, though not included in the model, that the NGOs will also attempt to influence other organizations such as analysts and the media which themselves have indirect influence over critical players. The NGOs attempt to influence the evaluations and actions of critical players by calling upon their interests, roles and responsibilities, values and norms.

The impact of NGOs' challenge on the critical players is mediated by, among other things, how they align or fail to align with the interests and institutional norms held by the critical players, beneficence of social and economic conditions for social movement efforts, and the degree of success in previous challenges by the NGO.

These challenges may generate responses by the firm. There may be a set of inter-organizational moves and counter-moves between the NGOs and the firm that take various forms such as provision of (mis)information, negotiations, threats and so forth. Furthermore, there could be efforts by the firm itself to influence the critical players to counter the effect of the NGO campaigns.

Ultimately, critical players may make evaluations and respond to the NGOs' "complaint" against the firm as well as the firm's defenses and counter-claims. Critical-player actions may generate economic losses by the firm and/or constraints on its behavior. Some of these losses – in the case of actions taken by critical players – can include costs associated with changes to the regulatory environment, reduced market size and market share, diminished brand value, shareholder constraints on behavior, lawsuits, work hold-ups, and often overlooked but perhaps of greatest importance, lowered employee morale. An example of this can be derived from Sir Mark Moody-Stuart, the former chairman of Shell. He said in an interview that the gravest impact of NGO campaigns against the oil giant were not on direct loss of sales or margin but on employee morale and the ability to attract and retain high-quality employees. NGO campaigns, particularly those pursuing more fundamental social change, can also alter the regulative rules of the game in which firms compete; NGO campaigns can lead to modifications in regulative oversight, legislation, taxation and subsidies.

The process of normative delegitimation turns on the dynamics associated with normative legitimacy. Two interrelated issues have been underemphasized in the existing literature on the dynamics surrounding a firm's legitimacy: the level of uncertainty and the broader social institutional demands placed upon firms. First, the external and distributed sources and control of legitimacy have the potential to generate a great deal of complexity in the firm's broader social environment,[14] which tends to increase state, effect and response uncertainty. The importance of the uncertainty associated with social legitimacy – with its less highly defined players, demands and dynamics relative to regulative legitimacy – has tended to be underdeveloped in the literature on legitimation pressure. Most of the literature – particularly in institutional theory – tends to assume away uncertainty and sees the fundamental problems of legitimacy as gaining legitimacy without an organizational history, or balancing conflicting institutional demands. All the while, the dramatic state of uncertainty surrounding sources, dynamics and impacts of potential legitimacy challenges is, for the most part, ignored.

Part of this underemphasis on uncertainty is also likely a cause and consequence of a second problem – the heavy focus on a limited set of institutional demands, particularly those concerning professionalism and "rationality." Theorists have rightly argued that these institutional concerns are central to business organizations, but the emphasis on this has led to an underemphasis on the broader social normative pressures on social movement organizations and the institutional values they represent. As the opening examples suggest, there seem to be growing social normative legitimating pressures brought to bear on firms in addition to the existing demands for professionalism and "rationality." A theory of social risk, with its intrinsic focus both on risk and on social normative legitimacy, should provide the emphasis and scope to address these shortcomings.

We now turn to briefly consider how the issue can be understood to build on the existing strategy literature by adding to the existing typology of firm risks.

Antecedents of social risk

In this section we present three sets of interacting factors – firm-related factors, institution-related factors and social movement factors – that drive a firm's social risk.

Firm-specific risk factors

Yaziji has identified a number of firm-specific risk factors and these have obvious managerial relevance.[15] We extend these factors here. Firms at the greatest social risk include those which:

1. **Offer life-saving, life-threatening or "socially sensitive" products** (e.g., pharmaceuticals, health care, arms and tobacco). Firms acting as a function of the industry in which they operate are subject to greater scrutiny because they produce socially sensitive products or services (e.g., "sin" industries such as alcohol, tobacco and pornography), operate in socially sensitive markets (children, the poor or uneducated, etc.), or both. Nestlé, for example, came under long-term challenge for selling baby formula in Third World countries where it was sometimes over-diluted in order to make the formula last longer, or mixed with non-potable water. It is easy for NGOs to cast these situations as "people versus profits."

2. **Confront changing social values** (e.g., fashion, media, alcohol, pornography, gambling). Firms that operate in environments of institutional flux or conflict are more likely to be drawn into a larger institutional battle. Firms in general should react to the social environment in which they operate to stay relevant to current times. If they do not respond to the external environment, or choose to capitalize on questionable practices during times of change, they are susceptible to NGO backlash. The example of TXU Corp. on p. 50 is an illustration of this challenge.

3. **Generate large externalities** (e.g., pollution, use of "commons" resources). The externalities are highly visible, may be dramatic and may be felt by a wide range of citizens and consumers, and thus campaigns are more likely to gain resources and garner support. Some firms, simply as a function of the industries in which they operate, generate more obvious externalities. This can be seen in heavy industries such as oil and power, waste management, heavy manufacturing and chemicals. These firms tend to face greater scrutiny by advocacy groups representing groups upon which the costs of these externalities fall.

4. **Have high power in a supply chain or market.** Firms such as Wal-Mart and Microsoft can often extract a high percentage of the surplus value in the supply chain. These firms are often seen as overly powerful, and competitors and other firms up and down the supply chain have an interest in reducing the power of the firm. As a result, NGO claims against the firm are more likely to find a positive reception among relevant third-party audiences.

5. **Have high brand awareness** (e.g., retail, clothing, food and beverage, automotive, media, finance). This awareness will itself be a

function of multiple factors such as firm size, closeness to final consumers and so forth. Public awareness increases the probability that an NGO will challenge a firm because attention has already been brought to potential issues. Furthermore, the overall salience of a firm to an NGO will also likely increase the probability of a challenge. It is efficient for NGOs to go after highly visible firms because they make easier targets insofar as the NGO does not need to expend resources introducing the firm to the public before challenging it in the court of public opinion. These firms make better targets for NGOs not only because they are already known to potential audiences of a campaign, but also because they are more easily cast as symbols of industries or institutions.

6. **Use new technologies** (e.g., genetic engineering, stem-cell-based research, personal-data collection). New technologies can raise new questions about whether the associated processes and products are legitimate and appropriate. Genetic modification of organisms, and more recently, nanotechnology, are inviting close scrutiny and challenge.

7. **Do business in different regions with differing ethical or social expectations** (e.g., virtually every multinational, particularly those operating in both developed and developing countries). Multinational corporations often face higher risk because they are subject to a greater number of institutional requirements, oftentimes experiencing conflicts within these requirements. Again, this touches upon the external social environments and subsequent agreement between the firm and the society in which it operates. As firms expand across borders, it becomes increasingly difficult to maintain core values and behave within acceptable realms in divergent environments.

8. **Are representative of controversial institutions (e.g., Capitalism, globalization, American culture).** Some firms might face greater social risk not because they are failing to conform to institutional standards – as is classically portrayed in most neo-institutional theory – but rather because they are exemplary representatives of an institution, whose own legitimacy is being challenged by NGOs. For example, some anti-globalization protestors have campaigned against McDonald's. While they identify a number of specific firm practices that they take to be egregious and especially harmful, they admit that their main reason for choosing McDonald's as a target is

because they take it to represent the institution of multinational corporations. One advocacy group, the McInformation Network, writes on its website, "Yes, we appreciate that McDonald's only sell hamburgers and loads of other corporations are just as bad. But that's not the point. They have been used as a symbol of all multinationals and big business relentlessly pursuing their profits at the expense of anything that stands in their way."[16] This form of campaign – which we call a "proxy campaign," will be covered in more detail in the next few chapters.

9. **Have the will and ability to withstand NGO challenges.** Firms may develop reputations as being *unwilling* to change their behavior in the face of NGO challenges and *capable of resisting* the pressure that these challenges create. For example, a firm may be able to resist NGO pressure if the NGO's perceptions of the firm's flagrant behaviors were not widely shared among critical players or if the firm had enough counter-influence to have these critical players continue to give their support to the firm. In such circumstances, NGOs may perceive further challenges as being in vain and turn their attention elsewhere. A comparison between ExxonMobil and Shell provides an illuminating example. ExxonMobil's general strategy has been one of resisting and ignoring NGOs whereas Shell has used strategies of appeasement, negotiation and cooperation. Though many environmental and social NGOs view ExxonMobil as having a worse approach to environmental and social concerns than Shell, NGOs tend to challenge Shell more than ExxonMobil simply because they gain more in their challenges to Shell. However, while the ability and intent to resist attacks may reduce their probability, NGOs may calculate that *if* they are to attack, the magnitude of the attack will need to be greater in order to overcome a powerful and resistant opponent.

10. **Are perceived to be egregious.** This refers to the extent to which the firm is perceived by NGOs to be more flagrant in its behavior with respect to those issues that are a concern to the NGOs (e.g., environment or social impact), relative to the firm's competitors that perform similar activities. For example, two oil extraction companies might be perceived to systematically have different impacts on the natural, social or political environments in the areas in which they drill; the firm perceived to act more egregiously

would increase the level of NGO dissatisfaction with its behavior and would also likely increase NGOs' assessment of the firm's vulnerability with respect to critical players' evaluations.

11. **Have poor organizational ability to perceive and respond to changing institutional demands.** Factors that promote organizational inertia and impede organizational change and adaptation will positively moderate the relationship between rate of institutional change and social risk since they impede the firm's ability to adapt to changing institutional demands. Such factors include organizational investments in fixed assets,[17] organizational coordination requirements[18] and individuals' preferences for consistency in their actions.[19]

Institutional risk factors

In addition to the firm-specific risk factors identified above, the institutional context is also relevant to a firm's exposure to social risk. This context affects the number of NGOs in a firm's environment, the relationship of demands placed on a firm by these NGOs, as well as the rate of change among these demands and the NGOs that represent them. In this section, we consider how competing and conflicting institutional demands, contested institutional dominance and rate of institutional change tend to increase a firm's social risk.

Competing institutional demands

Firms are simultaneously held to the demands of various institutions.[20] Meeting multiple sets of institutional requirements can place heavy strains on the limited resources of the firm, particularly when there is a great deal of "distance"[21] between the various institutions' demands. The higher the number of competing institutions under which a firm operates, the greater the number of social institutional demands it meets in order to gain or maintain legitimacy with NGOs representing the values of the various institutions. When more social demands are placed on the firm, it is more likely that the firm will fail to fully meet some of these demands and therefore face social challenges. Thus, the higher the number of institutions with competing demands under which the firm operates, the greater the probability of NGO challenges.

Conflicting institutional demands

An even more intractable situation is found when different institutions demand *mutually incompatible* behavior from the firm.[22] In such situations it is impossible for the firm to simultaneously fully meet the inherently incompatible demands placed upon it; satisfying one set of demands logically implies failing to meet another set of demands. Conflicting institutional demands can often arise in the context of pluralistic or liberal societies – as are found in much of the first world – and when a firm operates transnationally and thereby under the various institutions found across countries. For example, an American car assembly firm attempting to decide whether to close down its US factory and set up a *maquiladora* just south of the border will face a host of conflicting institutional pressures concerning the appropriateness of laying-off established American employees, maximizing shareholder return, meeting labor and environmental concerns, and so forth. In such a context of inherently conflicting institutional demands, the firm will almost certainly face some NGO challenge. Thus, the greater the conflict among institutions under which the firm operates, the greater the probability of NGO challenges.

Contested institutional dominance

A firm's social risk will also tend to be greater when it operates in an environment of contested institutional dominance – a situation in which there are active efforts by supporters of particular institutions to promote their institutions over those of others. Examples of such contestation for institutional dominance are the anti-globalization campaigns in which protestors introduce pressure for a fundamental change in the institutional environment. In such contexts of high-intensity institutional conflict, social challenges against firms are not always – even perhaps not often – based on the firm's being out of compliance with either generally accepted regulative or normative standards. That is, a focal firm's actions may be well aligned with established norms and values, yet still come under attack. NGOs that are dissatisfied with the institutional status quo may actively work to change it; the means employed may well involve attacks on organizations operating the given institution. Thus, the higher the degree of contestation between institutions for dominance, the greater the probability and magnitude of NGO challenges.

In addition we can expect a multiplicative interaction effect between, on the one hand, contestation of institutions for dominance and, on the other hand, a firm being exemplary of an institution under some degree of challenge.

Institutional change

The final institutional variable likely to have significant impact on a firm's social risk is the degree of institutional flux or the rate of institutional change. A dynamic institutional context – in which the demands of any given institution and the relative influence of the various institutions are shifting – is simply harder for an organization to understand and respond to than is a static one. Thus, the greater the rate of institutional change in a firm's environment, the greater will be the uncertainty of NGO challenges.

Social movement context

Social risk, as expressed through NGO campaigns, is also partially a function of the number and influence of NGOs. This, in turn, will partially be a function of the beneficence of the environment to the NGOs. As discussed in Chapter 2, social movement theory has identified a host of relevant factors affecting the hospitability of environments to social movements.

Four sets of macro, country-level factors – political, economic, social and technological – heavily influence the beneficence of the social context for social movements.

Political environment

The political environment affects the social movement opportunities within a nation.[23] The receptivity of the political system to organized protest, the rise of supportive elites, the evolution of sympathetic governmental agencies,[24] or the very structure of the political system[25] may all affect the degree of activism and the efficacy of protest. Some countries are more willing to allow challenges to firms than others. Laws concerning public association, libel, third-party lawsuits, for example, all affect the degree and ways in which NGOs can challenge firms, and influence the probability of success. In turn – using the backward-induction approach of game theory – this can shape the calculations of those NGOs weighing up whether or not to engage in active protest in the first place.

Economic environment

The most important economic driver of social movements is wealth. Wealth, at an individual and national level – perhaps surprisingly – positively correlates with the emergence and growth of social movements. Early theorists thought that deprived individuals would be most likely to protest, but the evidence suggests that those who are truly deprived rarely have the wherewithal to sustain a protest over time; general societal prosperity tends to correlate positively with social movement activity.[26] In addition to providing the economic reserves to pursue protest, wealth is associated with more rapid communication technologies (more on this below), the expansion of the intellectual classes and the development of new social technologies.[27]

Social environment

The organizational conditions in the society also affect the efficacy of social movements and thus likely also affect the social risk of firms. Two in particular seem to be relevant to the emergence and growth of social movements and will likely also be relevant to NGO challenges to firm legitimacy: the geographic concentration of individuals and movement members, and the level of prior organization. Geographic concentration such as in urban areas and university campuses greatly eases organization,[28] and the level of prior organization provides the infrastructure supportive of emerging movements.[29]

Technological environment

The final condition affecting the beneficence of the environment toward social movements is technology that enables protest. Particularly noteworthy of late have been the influences of communication technologies, such as email and the Internet, on social movements. These technologies have greatly empowered NGOs to gain information, reach their audiences and supporters, and quickly build issue-based alliances with one another.

Pulling these four sets of conditions together, we can provide the following summary statement of social movement related factors affecting social risk: the greater the political opportunities, wealth, organizational opportunities and social movement history, and enabling technologies of the environment, the greater will be the resources available to NGOs and thus the greater will be the firm's social risk.

Conclusion

As indicated in the opening paragraphs of this chapter, social risk represents a significant and growing unique phenomenon. Three developments suggest the trend will continue. First, communication technologies such as email and the Internet are becoming increasingly ubiquitous, thereby increasing the range of influence of NGOs and thus the reach of social demands across previously isolated institutional fields. This same technology is allowing greater opportunities for coordinated efforts among NGOs within and across borders. Second, as firms increasingly operate transnationally, they will inevitably expose themselves to competing and conflicting demands. Third, the ongoing spread of liberal and democratic regimes[30] tends to improve the social movement context, thereby strengthening NGOs. This spread of democracy also increases the competition and conflict among institutions; as one author notes, in liberal, pluralistic societies, inconsistent and contesting institutional frameworks are commonplace.[31] While this dynamic introduces more challenges for many organizations, it enhances the notion that NGOs have a significant role in society, and they are far from realizing the end of their days.

Notes

1 P. Drucker, "Will the corporation survive?" *Economist* November 3 (2001), 15.
2 R. Vernon, *In The Hurricane's Eye* (Cambridge, MA: Harvard University Press, 1998).
3 M. C. Suchman, "Managing legitimacy: Strategic and institutional approaches," *Academy of Management Review* 20 (3) (1995), 571–610.
4 P. Selznick, *Leadership in Administration* (Berkeley: University of California Press, 1957).
5 R. W. Scott, *Institutions and Organizations* (Thousand Oaks: Sage, 2001).

6 For example, H. E. Aldrich and C. M. Fiol, "Fools rush in? The institutional context of industry creation," *Academy of Management Review* 19 (4) (1994), 645–670; C. Oliver, "Strategic responses to institutional processes," *Academy of Management Review* 16 (1991), 145–197; Suchman, "Managing legitimacy," 571–610; M. A. Zimmerman and G. J. Zeitz, "Beyond survival: Achieving new venture growth by building legitimacy," *Academy of Management Review* 27 (3) (2002), 414–431.

7 T. D'Aunno, R. I. Sutton and R. H. Price, "Isomorphism and external support in conflicting institutional environments: A study of drug abuse treatment units," *Academy of Management Journal* 34 (3) (1991), 636–661; T. Kostova and S. Zaheer, "Organizational legitimacy under conditions of complexity: The case of the multinational enterprise," *Academy of Management Review* 24 (1) (1999), 64–81; M. Ruef and R. W. Scott, "A multidimensional model of organizational legitimacy: Hospital survival in changing institutional environments," *Administrative Science Quarterly* 43 (4) (1998), 877–904.

8 See Scott, *Institutions and Organizations* for a thorough review.

9 C. Oliver, "Strategic responses to institutional processes," *Academy of Management Review* 16 (1991), 145–179.

10 W. Thorngate, "Possible limits on a science of social behavior," in L. H. Strickland, F. E. Aboud and K. J. Gergen (eds.), *Social Psychology in Transition* (New York: Plenum, 1976), pp. 121–139; K. E. Weick, "What theory is *not*, theorizing *is*," *Administrative Science Quarterly* 40 (3) (1995), 385–390.

11 These advocacy organizations are often referred to as nongovernmental organizations (NGOs) in the popular press. While there is an overlap between social movement organizations (SMOs) and NGOs, SMOs which generate social risk may or may not be nonprofit and NGOs will include non risk-inducing organizations such as churches, charity groups, etc. Despite this imperfect overlap, it is worth noting the growth in influence of SMOs as suggested by the twenty-fold increase in citations of "NGO" or "nongovernmental organization" in the *Wall Street Journal* and the *Financial Times* (often in the context of the organization challenging firm or industry behavior) in the last ten years.

12 J. Frooman, "Stakeholder influence strategies," *Academy of Management Review* 24 (1999), 191–205.

13 M. Garguilo, "Two-step leverage: Managing constraint in organizational politics," *Administrative Science Quarterly* 38 (1) (1993), 1–19.

14 D. Stark, "Recombinant property in East European capitalism," *American Journal of Sociology* 101 (4) (1996), 993–1027.

15 M. Yaziji, "Turning gadflies into allies," *Harvard Business Review*, February (2004), 110–115.

16 www.mcspotlight.org/help.html. December 2002.

17 M. T. Hannan and J. Freeman, "The population ecology of organizations," *American Journal of Sociology* 82 (5) (1977), 929–964.

18 D. Miller and P. H. Friesen, "Momentum and revolution in organizational adaptation," *Academy of Management Journal* 23 (4) (1980), 591–614.

19 B. M. Staw, "The escalation of commitment to a course of action," *Academy of Management Review* 6 (4) (1981), 577–587.

20 D'Aunno, Sutton and Price, "Isomorphism and external support," 636–661; D. L. Deephouse, "Does isomorphism legitimate?" *Academy of Management Journal* 39 (4) (1996), 1024–1039; J. W. Meyer, R. W. Scott and D. Strang, "Centralization, fragmentation, and school district complexity," *Administrative Science Quarterly* 32 (1987), 186–201; W. W. Powell, "Institutional effects on organizational structure and performance," in L. G. Zucker (ed.), *Institutional Patterns and Organizations: Culture and Environment* (Cambridge, MA: Ballinger, 1988), pp. 115–136; Ruef and Scott, "A multidimensional model of organizational legitimacy," 877–904.

21 Kostova and Zaheer, "Organizational legitimacy," 64–81.

22 D'Aunno, Sutton and Price, "Isomorphism and external support," 636–661.

23 P. Eisinger, "The conditions of protest behavior in American cities," *American Political Science Review* 67 (1973), 11–28; J. C. Jenkins and C. Perrow, "Insurgency of the powerless: Farm workers' movements (1946–1972)," *American Sociological Review* 42 (1977), 249–268.

24 R. Gale, "Social movements and the state: The environmental movement, countermovement, and government agencies," *Sociological Perspectives* 29 (1986), 202–240.

25 D. Nelkin and M. Pollak, *The Atom Besieged* (Cambridge, MA: MIT Press, 1981).

26 D. McAdam, J. D. McCarthy and M. N. Zald, "Social movements," in N. Smelser (ed.), *Handbook of Sociology* (Newbury Park: Sage, 1988), pp. 695–737.

27 M. N. Zald and J. D. McCarthy, "Organizational intellectuals and the criticism of society," *Social Service Review* 49 (1975), 344–362.

28 J. D'Emilio, *Sexual Politics, Sexual Communities* (Chicago: University of Chicago Press, 1983).

29 J. Freeman, "The origins of the women's liberation movement," *American Journal of Sociology* 78 (1973), 792–811; A. Morris, *The Origins of the Civil Rights Movement* (New York: Free Press, 1984).
30 A. Karatnycky, *Freedom in the World: The Annual Survey of Political Rights and Civil Liberties 2001–2002* (New York: Freedom House, 2002).
31 Scott, *Institutions and Organizations*.

5 | *How do they do it? Understanding the power and influence of radical advocacy NGOs*[1]

The phenomenon of NGO campaigns against corporations are highly complex and cross multiple levels of analysis. NGOs are themselves constrained and enabled by the group processes and internal resource dependencies of the organization and its supporters. These group processes within the organization affect the strategic behavior of these NGOs in terms of tactic and target selection and strategic interactions between the NGO and the targeted firm at both organizational and inter-organizational levels. These inter-organizational dynamics that make up the campaign ultimately are evaluated by third-party individuals who evaluate the various claims made by both the NGO and the targeted firm. At the individual-level, they may adjust their beliefs and thereby collectively affect the legitimacy and strength of competing institutional frameworks at the society-level.

The radical NGO paradox

Extreme advocacy or "radical" NGOs are, by definition, working against the mainstream of their societies – either in terms of values and beliefs or in terms of regulatory systems – and fundamentally aim for change. As such, radical NGOs, at first blush, should not be very effective, particularly in proxy war campaigns. First, the more radical the NGO, the smaller it is likely to be and the fewer resources it is likely to be able to draw upon since it is out of the mainstream in terms of ideology and will therefore have fewer people and organizations that will be willing to support it.

Second, in a proxy war, the goal of the NGO is to change the dominant institution represented by the targeted firm. Institutions, on the other hand, are highly resistant to change. They are stable social structures consisting of logics – beliefs, norms and values that guide practical action – and governance structures through which power

74

and authority are exercised.[2] In fact, for decades sociologists detailed and emphasized just how impervious institutions are to change.[3]

How then can institutional change take place – and especially be driven by small, resource poor, ideologically radical NGOs – when dominant institutional logics, governance systems and resources are all stacked to favor the status quo? Despite all of the factors stacked up against radical NGOs, they are actually surprisingly effective. In fact, in the empirical research that Yaziji conducted, he found that when controlling for size, the more radical the NGO, the more effective it tended to be![4] This runs totally counter to most of the logic underlying organizational theory as well as institutional theory. So how to explain this paradox?

As such, we address this paradox by focusing on how NGOs strategically leverage institutional factors to generate political opportunities for institutional change. We present a theoretical explanation, grounded in neo-institutional theory and resource dependency theory (discussed in Chapter 4), as well as empirical data in support of these theories. We explain the benefits that actually accrue to more radical NGOs and how these increase the efficacy of these ideologically radical organizations in their efforts to change the dominant institutions. In particular, we will introduce the notion of *institutionally circumscribed resource niches* and suggest how a single narrow institutional resource niche provides institution-challenging NGOs with an advantage over larger, more mainstream organizations saddled with the constraints and costs imposed by institutions that give voice to every represented group.

Resource pools

The key to answering these practical and theoretical mysteries is in terms of institutionally circumscribed resource pools. In their classic book, *The External Control of Organizations*, Pfeffer and Salancik highlight how organizations are dependent on multiple stakeholders for the resources necessary to keep the organization functioning.[5] Each resource provider has its own motivations for providing resources. For example, suppliers interact with a firm in order to generate sales, customers are willing to provide cash to access the products and services of the firm, employees will provide their labor for a salary and shareholders and bondholders will provide capital in

exchange for ownership or interest payments. These various constraints encountered by organizations are termed *resource-dependencies* in Pfeffer and Salancik's framework.

We can conceptually divide up the resource pools that are potentially available to the focal organization in terms of the motivations or
interests of the potential resource providers. For example, organizations that can generate a certain product type at a certain price will
have access to a potential pool of resources – in this case money –
from the customers in the relevant market segment. Similarly if the
firm has a certain risk rating and offers a certain rate of return, it will
have access to a pool of resources associated with potential bondholders of the firm. Furthermore, if the firm seems to have a bright
future, it will have access to the pool of resources controlled by a
certain segment of potential shareholders.

If one asks about the motivations that resource providers such as
volunteers or donors have to NGOs, the most obvious answers will
directly or indirectly relate to the fact that the NGO is pursuing goals
that are in line with those of the resource provider. For example,
volunteers for the Red Cross likely volunteer at least in part because
they support the goals of the Red Cross. Thus, in addition to things
such as access to financial returns or access to an organization's
products, another motivation to contribute resources can be based on
shared values, such as institutional or ideological alignment.

We can think of pools of resources as being attached to particular
institutional value sets, such that these resources are preferentially
available to those organizations that conform or promote a given
institutional value set. We shall define these as institutionally circumscribed resource pools.

The resource pools of radical NGOs and corporations

Let's turn again to the resources that radical NGOs are likely to
access. Most of these NGOs do not have significant sales of products
or services and are not, primarily, economic actors. Most of the
benefits that they will tend to provide to resource providers will
directly or indirectly be linked to the values of the NGO and how
the NGO represents and furthers these values. That is, most of
the potential resources will be best understood as institutionally

circumscribed resources, or fundamentally driven by values and norms. For example, some people who feel very strongly about the rights and welfare of animals might give money and effort to PETA. Other people, who have a different set of values, and who have no strong feelings about the welfare of animals will not provide resources to PETA.

Resource pools and organizational ideology

The notion of resources pools as institutionally circumscribed is intimately linked to the traditional institutional perspective in which the organization-as-institution is a locus and source of shared norms and values for its members.[6] Through socialization and internalization, members of the organization assume the norms, values and evaluative perspective of the organization. While these values and norms can concern rather mundane issues of correct processes and structures of the organization, they can also concern broader social, political and economic issues and values. In this perspective, an organization's norms, values and evaluative judgments can be considered to be the organization's *ideology*.

While definitions of "ideology" differ, John Wilson's non-pejorative, widely referenced definition will be adopted here: ideology is understood to be "a set of beliefs about the social world and how it operates, containing statements about the rightness of certain social arrangements and what action would be undertaken in light of those statements . . . An ideology is both a cognitive map of sets of expectations and a scale of values in which standards and imperatives are proclaimed."[7] As such, ideologies refer to three main beliefs: beliefs about how the world operates, the moral appropriateness of the current arrangements, and what should be done to bring these two into alignment.[8]

In the context of applying ideologies at the organizational level, they operate as beliefs and values about political, social and economic issues as well as beliefs about the importance of various factors as solutions to the focal issues of the organization. These factors can range from better enforcement of existing regulations, through minor and major modifications to the rules, to fundamental changes to basic aspects of the political, economic or social system.

Radicalism

Based on the above definition, *organizational ideological radicalism* can be understood as the extent to which an organization's beliefs and values about a given focal issue are out of alignment with the dominant institutions of its societal system, which is often coextensive with the state. The less alignment, the more radical the ideology. As such, radicalism is relative both to the issue itself as well as to the society in which this issue evolves. Relative to *issues*, an organization can be ideologically radical in terms of one focal issue, but mainstream in terms of another. For instance, the Animal Liberation Front is ideologically radical in the US in terms of its values with regards to animal rights, but it is ideologically mainstream or even neutral with regard to, say, wealth distribution in society, or gender issues. Relative to *society,* radicalism is necessarily comparable to the organization's reference society. For example, the Socialist Party in the US is more ideologically radical (relative to the beliefs and values of the US-at-large) than is the Socialist Party in Serbia (relative to the beliefs and values of Serbia-at-large).

In the following paragraphs, we focus on "ideologically driven organizations," as opposed to "interest-driven organizations." We define ideologically driven organizations as those in which the primary goal is an "other"-oriented private good or a public good of which very little is owned, shared, captured or distributed by the contributors, members and owners of the organization. This can be contrasted with "interest-driven" organizations, where the primary goal of the organization is the creation of private goods that are distributed among the contributors, members and owners of the organization. An example of a radical ideologically driven advocacy NGO is the Sweatshop Watch, whose main goal is improvement of labor conditions in textile factories in the developing world, and whose members are almost exclusively in the developed world and not employed in textile industries. In the case of ideology-driven efforts, contributors' motivations lie in investing in an ideological goal that extends beyond personal self-interest. Efforts and contributions are made on the basis of both values as well as sentiments.

Cognitive and emotional drivers for NGO activities

Ideological radicalism – consisting of norms, values and beliefs, is essentially cognitive in nature, with both descriptive (how things are) and normative (how things ought to be) content. But organizational ideological radicalism cannot be reduced to these rational or cognitive processes, as it is also fundamentally driven by an *emotional* component, ideological fervor, which can be defined as the intensity of the emotion or sentiment toward a set of social, economic or political issues.

Ideological fervor plays a crucial role in ideologically driven organizations in attracting and maintaining resources by ensuring motivation and sustained effort from the labor force and financial donors. We can conceive of organizational ideological fervor simply as the average of individual members' ideological fervor toward the focal social, economic or political issues of the organization.[9]

Other-benefitting NGOs, as discussed in Chapter 1, face the fundamental challenge of attracting capital and labor to support their effort. The main aim of such organizations is to produce other-oriented or public goods. The *beneficiaries* of the good and the *contributors* to the good may be mutually exclusive; for example, "liberated" lab animals are not the PETA members who "liberate" them. Often there are no "paying customers." The beneficiaries do not provide economic compensation to the contributors for their efforts. Why then do contributors contribute? Ideological fervor functions as a crucial means by which these organizations gain capital and labor contributions. Contributions are attracted not based on a promise of financial payoff, nor by exclusively appealing to rational arguments, but above all through ideological fervor channeled into effort through the organization.

In this case, other-oriented sentiments are the solution to Olson's famous problem of free riding and collective action.[10] Olson's focus was on the difficulty of attracting effort toward a collective good when the individual's access to the collective good is relatively independent of the individual's effort toward achieving the collective good. In ideologically driven organizations, the other-directed good sought by the organization will not offset the efforts of the contributors, even if all potential contributors did, in fact, contribute.[11]

In the sections below we consider how ideological radicalism may affect the institutionally proactive behavior of advocacy organizations in campaigning against corporations.

Radicalism and homogeneity

There are a number of reasons to believe that the degree of ideological radicalism of the organization will affect the degree of ideological alignment of the resource providers of the organization. Radical NGOs tend to have a relatively small institutionally circumscribed resource pool from which to draw. This is because the willingness to provide resources to these organizations is based on particular, and limited, institutional value sets. Most of the institutionally circumscribed resources in the organization's environment are likely to be withheld from radical NGOs, since most of the individuals and organizations that control these resources will be hesitant to provide resources to organizations with which they have dichotomous ideological viewpoints.

As such, organizational radicalism, while foreclosing support from the vast majority of resources which are available to more mainstream organizations, tends to increase the ideological homogeneity of the resource providers it does manage to attract. There are a number of reasons for this. First, the more radical the organization, the greater the social sanction associated with providing resources to the organization. For example, providing labor to the Environmental Liberation Front, which burns SUVs and houses in environmentally sensitive areas, will expose the labor provider to social reproach as well as legal sanction. Thus, there is an especially strong self-selection mechanism for resource providers of radical organizations. They will only help out if they are strongly aligned philosophically with the organization *and* are driven by sufficient ideological fervor to be willing to incur the potentially resulting sanctions.

Second, supporters of radical organizations tend to feel they are engaged in a David versus Goliath battle, and they will tend to have a high level of "us-against-them" thinking. This can foster groupthink as well as in-group versus out-group social processes,[12] and thus minimize any philosophical differences among the supporters. In short, they will tend to close ranks ideologically in the face of the opposition.

Third, it is likely that supporters will further identify with the organization under these conditions. An identity can be seen as a set of logically connected propositions that a person uses to describe himself/herself to himself/herself or others.[13] Klandersmans used such an approach to argue that social movement organizations can develop a collective identity that expresses their shared interests and goals.[14] This collective identification thus adds to ideological fervor towards functioning as a basis for individual commitment and sense of solidarity.[15]

Finally, radical organizations simply tend to be smaller and thus have fewer dependencies. Since resources are usually provided in "lumps," there will be a tendency to have fewer resource providers. Mathematically, this will tend to decrease the chance for ideological conflict among the resource providers.

In sum, we can expect that most radical NGOs will tend to be small and resource poor, but ideologically homogeneous with a passionate base of supporters. Indeed, this is what we often find to be the case. Using employee count or revenues as a guideline, even the largest, most moderate NGOs are miniscule in comparison to the largest multinationals, for example WWF versus Google. These NGOs are not significant economic players and thus do not have access to such resource pools as potential employees, debt holders, shareholders and customers which are available to successful economic organizations.

The inability to garner significant resources from outside organizations interested in economic returns or in tangible products of the radical NGO will limit them to the small niches that are controlled by individuals or organizations that share their ideology and support the institutional change being pursued by the NGO. In other terms, more radical NGOs will have access to much smaller institutionally circumscribed resources pools than the moderate NGOs due to the incongruous beliefs between the institution and the radical NGO. We see this to be the case in instances such as when Black Block, the Earth Liberation Front and other radical organizations tend to be quite small compared to more mainstream NGOs such as WWF, Amnesty International and Ducks Unlimited. In sum, *the greater the ideological radicalism of an NGO, the greater will be the institutional homogeneity of its resource providers.*

Homogeneity of resource providers as a source of organizational freedom

In the section above we discussed the fact that the radical NGO is dedicated to undermining a dominant institution. Although limiting the pool of available resources, the radical NGO has a relatively institutionally homogeneous set of individuals and organizations upon which it is resource dependent. Given the wide ideological range of possible organizations to which they could contribute, the suppliers of capital and labor to a particular radical NGO will tend to be relatively homogeneous in their support of the ideological goals and institutional value sets of the NGO. If their views diverge from that of the NGO, they can easily direct their resources elsewhere.

In contrast, the corporations that the radical NGOs target are usually gigantic organizations, fulfilling multiple functions in more than one country for a large number of stakeholders. The mere size of the throughput, in terms of labor, capital and resources, ensures a vast set of resource dependencies. The fact that the corporation is driven primarily by practical rather than political ends also allows for greater institutional heterogeneity in the resources upon which it is dependent. Employees, customers and suppliers, for example, could believe in very different ideologies, but deal with the corporation for practical, self-interested and economic reasons.

Thus, the truism in organizational theory that most organizations exist in a context of institutional complexity, applies more to large corporations than to small radical NGOs. Accordingly, the conflicting demands placed on these larger corporations operating in institutionally complex fields are more severe for corporations than for the NGOs that campaign against them. In other terms, NGOs benefit from substantially higher levels of organizational freedom as opposed to the enemy they are confronting.

Radicalism, homogeneity and impact

As discussed, we can think of pools of resources as being attached to particular institutions, such that these resources are preferentially available to those organizations that conform to the given institution's demands. In the prior section, we defined institutional homogeneity of resource providers (or "homogeneity" for ease of reference) as the degree to which resource providers share common institutional norms and values, or the extent to which they are in the same institutional "niche."

NGOs therefore are working against the mainstream values and beliefs of their societies.

Homogeneity yields impact

Above, we discussed how a given NGO's radicalism tends to increase the institutional homogeneity of its resource providers, and thereby provide greater organizational freedom. Now let us examine how homogeneity can increase impact as well. Organizations are constrained in their actions. In addition to internal constraints generated and sustained by conflicting coalitions and interests within the organization,[16] there are also external constraints as a function of the multiple resource dependencies to which an organization is subject.[17] The limits or restrictions on organizational behavior are a function of the contradictory demands of various individuals, groups or outside organizations upon which the focal organization depends.

We see how ideological homogeneity of resource providers reduces the conflicting demands placed on an organization and thus increases its possible range of action. This, in turn, increases the efficacy or impact of the organization. In the case of NGOs, their impact is measured in terms of their effects on a targeted firm. In Michael Yaziji's research this measure ranged from: (a) the campaign had no real effect on the firm, (b) the campaign harmed the firm's reputation, (c) the firm made symbolic changes to its behavior, (d) the firm made substantive changes to its behavior, and (e) the attitude of the firm changed.[18]

Of course, ideological homogeneity does not ensure total freedom of action for the organization. First, resource providers can share similar ideologies but have different and conflicting interests. In cases in which interests are much more influential than ideologies, homogeneity of ideologies will likely have little effect, whereas alignment of interests would have a larger effect.

In cases in which the ideologies of resource providers have a real impact on organizational behavior, completely homogenous ideologies do not allow total freedom of action for the organization. Specifically, organizational actions which conflict with the dominant ideology will likely never even reach serious consideration, let alone garner the support necessary for implementation. For example, the American Civil Liberties Union (ACLU), which fights for freedom of expression, would not likely be able to publicly burn the US Patriot Act as a form of protest against it. The tactic simply runs counter to the values of the organization and its providers.

Nonetheless, there are reasons to believe that ideological homogeneity would serve to increase the freedom and impact of an organization's actions. Greater ideological homogeneity would tend to increase employee/volunteer cohesion, group identification and effort. Organizations will tend to face fewer constraints on types of actions or tactics that can be employed, would be freer in the actions open to them and thus could engage in more vigorous, undiluted actions.

In the context of NGOs campaigning against firms to bring the firm into line with existing expectations we can see them as functioning in a sort of proxy war to change institutions. Furthermore, the greater the institutional homogeneity of an NGO's resource providers, the greater will be the NGO's effect on institutions, as well as its effect on firms.

Let's consider an example of how NGOs are able to leverage their small but homogeneous resource niche to forcefully attack the corporation whose response is constrained by its institutionally heterogeneous resource dependencies. For example, NGOs campaigned against pharmaceutical companies for their pricing and patent enforcement efforts in South Africa. Some NGOs were created in response to this very issue. The NGOs did not have to worry about losing support from their capital and labor providers over the goals of the campaign. The individuals and organizations upon which the NGOs were dependent were virtually unanimous in their ideological stance on the issue. Their position was united and unequivocal.

In contrast, the pharmaceutical corporations under attack were speaking simultaneously to multiple, separate constituencies including the South African government, developed world consumers, South African, American and British NGOs, trans-governmental organizations responsible for international patent agreements and financial analysts. These audiences had a wide range of worldviews and values – as well as interests – and the pharmaceutical companies had great difficulty in addressing or sidestepping the conflicting demands. The institutional ideologies of patents and shareholder capitalism came into direct conflict with ideologies of the pre-eminence of public health concerns. The corporations – burdened with the conflicting demands of various stakeholders and aggressive NGOs that were demanding explicit action – vacillated ineffectively in their response. For example, the corporations filed a lawsuit against the South African government to enforce their patent – explicitly out of concern for the institution of patents, rather than immediate concern about profits – only to drop the suit six weeks later when further NGO pressure was exerted. The greater institutional complexity of firms relative to that of NGOs underlies the need for multivocality and thereby limits the

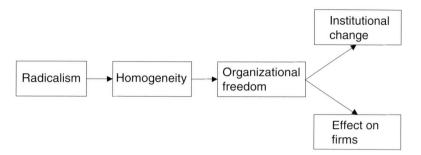

Figure 5.1 Radicalism, homogeneity and impact

options for both responding to conflicting institutional pressures as well as the possibility of being institutionally entrepreneurial. NGOs do not experience this same lack of organizational freedom and are thus left with a larger repertoire of organizational action in order to pursue their goals.

The above theoretical links concerned institutional homogeneity of resource providers, organizational freedom and the ability and efficacy of organizations to pursue institutional change, as illustrated in Figure 5.1. In the remainder of this chapter we extend this thinking by studying the relationship between organizational ideological radicalism and the institutional homogeneity of resource providers. We quote research that confirms the causal chain linking organizational ideology, through homogeneity of resource providers to tactics, target selection and efficacy.

Radicalism and tactic selection

Tactics can be described by the degree to which they use existing political, legal and regulatory institutions to attain the ends sought, and how broadly accepted they are within the community-at-large. For instance, lawsuits, lobbying of regulators and lobbying of politicians are tactics which can be described as "highly institutional" or "institution-dependent" along this dimension. Press conferences, rallies and marches might be considered "institutionally neutral" in that they rely less on political, legal and regulatory institutions, but do not contravene these institutions. Finally, civil disobedience, direct action to disrupt businesses and streets, destruction of property and violence

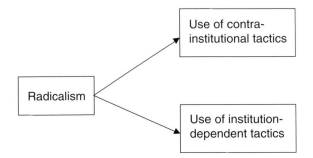

Figure 5.2 Radicalism and tactic selection

are all tactics which, generally being illegal, contravene institutions and can be labeled contra-institutional. Figure 5.2 shows the relationship between radicalism and tactics that can be used. Discovering the ability and ultimate goal of the radical NGO allows for a better understanding as to how institutionalized the actions will be, and what tactics might be used to reach their goals.

Tactics can be used in two ways. A contra-institutional method uses tactics that conflict in some way with institutional expectations, e.g., boycotts, civil disobedience, direct action or destruction of property. An institution-dependent method uses tactics that depend on major institutions, in this case the courts, the legislature and executive, and regulators, e.g., lobbying of regulators and politicians.

There are problems with this typology of tactics, but it does capture significant differences across them. Perhaps the first problem is that it is not clear what counts as an institution. For example, press conferences use the media, which could be considered a social, though not governmental, institution. A second problem is that one could reasonably argue that some of the tactics described as contra-institutional, such as civil disobedience, are actually highly ritualized and institutionalized and those engaging in civil disobedience use the police forces to help them make their point. Part of the problem is in the nature of the phenomenon itself; the exact nature of institutions is subject to multiple definitions as are the boundaries of any institution given a particular definition. In defense of these distinctions, even though there is some arbitrariness to exactly where the lines are drawn, the distinctions are significant insofar as they capture intuitions and allow us to have finer-grained understanding of the phenomenon.

Contra-institutional tactics have a number of attributes that make them more attractive as an option for ideologically radical organizations than for ideologically mainstream or moderate organizations. First, these tactics tend to be less resource-demanding. An individual or group of people, with little or no training or capital or networks, can engage in civil disobedience, direct action and violence. By contrast, political and regulative lobbying, for example, tends to require established networks among institutional players such as politicians and regulators. Radical organizations, at odds with the dominant institutions, might be less inclined to have these networks than mainstream or moderate organizations. To the extent that radical organizations are often relatively resource-poor in terms of capital and networks into the dominant institutions, radical tactics become relatively more attractive.

Positive feedback systems will tend to enforce this mechanism, as the use of radical tactics may tend to isolate the radical organization from more mainstream sources of capital as well as from key players in the dominant institutions. The mainstream holders of capital and individuals ensconced in highly institutionalized networks have their own resource-dependencies, which are likely also within the dominant institutions, and thus will tend to avoid jeopardizing their own legitimacy within their field by providing support to radical organizations.

Mainstream and moderate NGOs will tend to have more access to – and, importantly, reliance on – resources housed within the dominant institutional context, and thus will tend to avoid legitimacy-threatening contra-institutional tactics. Radical organizations being less reliant on these dominant-institution resources will be free to pursue these radical tactics.

So how do NGOs know how institutionalized their actions should be? Figure 5.3 illustrates the interconnections between actions and the

Highly institutionalized						Barely institutionalized
Political and regulatory lobbying	Leafleting	Protests and marches	Civil disobedience	Direct action inhibiting business practices	Destruction of property	Violence
Lawsuits						

Figure 5.3 Radicalism and degree of institutionalization

level to which institutionalization occurs. The NGO must perform within means, and once a tactic is chosen and a course is put into place, the level of institutionalization is clear.

Radicalism and target selection

The degree of ideological radicalism of an advocacy NGO affects its choice of target, i.e. the direction of institutional pressure generated by the NGO. In this subsection we will distinguish the targets and purposes of campaigns by mainstream, moderate and radical organizations. Mainstream advocacy organizations, being ideologically in harmony with the dominant institutions of their environments, will tend to be institutionally conservative, resisting institutional change and/or being a source of normative pressure for isomorphism.

The ideological bearing among advocacy organizations will have implications for which corporations they target. Ideologically mainstream organizations – engaging in "watchdog campaigns" (see Chapters 1 and 6) – will tend to target those organizations that fail to sufficiently conform to dominant institutional standards of appropriate behavior. This includes the values and norms that characterize the prevailing ideology in a given society. Generally the goal in such campaigns is to convince the critical, institutionally mainstream players that the target is in violation of broadly accepted normative or regulative standards. In the case of alleged normative violations, appeals to emotion or conscience will often be employed. In cases of alleged regulative violations, a more legalistic argument will have to be made concerning questions of fact and law. Common examples of such campaigns are those by local NGOs using the courts or the regulatory bodies to enforce existing and well-understood and accepted laws. For example, a local group might sue for an injunction against the opening of a liquor store within 500 feet of a school.

Moderate organizations, having the goal of moderate institutional change, will tend more than mainstream organizations to target corporations as a means of highlighting to a broader audience why the dominant institution needs moderate adjustment. A classic example of this type of campaign was the campaign started by Ralph Nader's book *Unsafe at Any Speed* which primarily targeted

GeneralMotors and its Corvair. As is described on one of Nader's websites:

The chief target of the book was General Motors' "sporty" Corvair, whose faulty rear suspension system made it possible to skid violently and roll over. The corporate negligence that had produced the various Corvair defects, said Nader, was "one of the greatest acts of industrial irresponsibility in the present century." More generally, Nader's book documented how Detroit habitually subordinated safety to style and marketing concerns.[19]

In such campaigns where the goal is moderate institutional change, the targeted corporation is used as a case-in-point of why common industry practices need to change, because they are out of compliance with either normative or regulative institutional norms or values. A common rhetorical tactic is to extend extreme examples as being representative of a more general phenomenon. Thus, moderate organizations will also tend to target corporations that demonstrate most vividly the implied normative or regulative violations.

Finally, ideologically radical advocacy organizations, interested in fundamental institutional change, will be more likely than either mainstream or moderate organizations to target corporations, not because they fail to conform to dominant institutional standards, *but precisely because they do.* For example, The Environmental Liberation Front and the Animal Liberation Front are organized in cells that engage in extensive property destruction. Black Block, which describes itself as "a group of anarchists and anarchist affinity groups," engages in destruction of property as a form of direct action. Targets are often chosen for highlighting the problematic aspect of the institutional system.

Taken together, the above discussion highlights how the degree of ideological radicalism will influence the criteria by which advocacy organizations choose the targets of their campaigns. In summary, it appears that when NGOs select their corporations to target, the more ideologically radical the advocacy organization, the more heavily they will weigh the degree to which the corporation is seen by the advocacy organization as representative of fundamental political, social or economic institutions. Overall, NGOs have a multifaceted approach to combining their goals, targets and tactics. Oftentimes, the degree of radicalism depends on how rational or emotional the community is

	Mainstream	Moderate	Radical
Goals	Enforcement of existing laws and norms	Small change to institutions/ laws or their interpretation	Major change to central tenants of dominant institutions
Target	Violators of laws	"Bad boys" representing the "worst" of the dominant institutions (case-in-point)	Symbols of dominant institutions
Tactics	Use of dominant institutions of enforcements (e.g., police, courts) Less emotional, more rational appeal	Use of dominant institutions that define and refine the laws and norms (e.g., courts, legislators, regulatory bodies) and appeal to public opinion (institution-independent tactics e.g., use of media, demonstrations, etc.)	Counter-institutional tactics attempting to reshape public opinion Emotional appeal

Figure 5.4 Radicalism and selection of goals, targets and tactics

when it comes to NGO actions. Figure 5.4 illustrates this multidimensional outline.

Conclusions

This chapter has illustrated how a single narrow institutional resource niche provides institutional challengers, such as NGOs, with an advantage over dominant organizations saddled with the constraints and costs imposed by institutional multivocality. Radical organizations, while at a disadvantage relative to more mainstream organizations, avoid these constraints and increase their freedom of action through the homogeneity of their resource providers. This homogeneity increases their range of tactical options and ideological arguments in their campaigns for institutional change. Thus we have the highly counter-intuitive insight that radical organizations actually have an institutional source of strength in their radicalism.

The chapter also highlights the strategic considerations of organizations responsible for institutional pressure and institutional change. While there is a great deal of literature on how organizations manage institutional pressure, institutional pressure itself is often considered diffuse and "impersonal." In contrast, this chapter touches on the strategic considerations of some of the organizations responsible for institutional pressure.

Notes

1 This chapter is derived from the theoretical and empirical work of Michael Yaziji's dissertation, "Institutional change and social risk: A study of campaigns by social movement organizations against firms," INSEAD (2004).

2 R. W. Scott, *Institutions and Organizations* (Thousand Oaks: Sage, 2001).

3 See, for example, P. J. Dimaggio and W. W. Powell, "The iron cage revisited: Institutional isomorphism and collective rationality in organizational fields," *American Sociological Review* 48 (1983), 147–160 for some of the isomorphic forces supporting institutional persistence.

4 M. Yaziji, "Turning gadflies into allies," *Harvard Business Review* 82 (2) (2004), 110–115.

5 J. Pfeffer and G. R. Salancik, *The External Control of Organizations: A Resource Dependence Perspective* (New York: Harper and Row, 1978).

6 P. Selznick, *Leadership in Administration* (Berkeley: University of California Press, 1957).

7 J. Wilson, *Introduction to Social Movements* (New York: Basic Books, 1973), pp. 91–92.

8 Wilson, *Introduction to Social Movements*, pp. 91–92.

9 See J. R. Kelly and S. G. Barsade, "Mood and emotions in small groups and work teams," *Organizational Behavior and Human Decision Processes* 86 (1) (2001) for a defense of group-level emotion constructs.

10 M. Olson Jr., *The Logic of Collective Action: Public Goods and the Theory of Groups* (Cambridge: Harvard University Press, 1965).

11 It is worth noting that the organizational or individual pursuit of other-oriented goods does not contradict the economic view of human behavior (K. J. Arrow, "Gifts and exchanges," *Philosophy and Public Affairs* Summer (1) (1972), 343–362; G. S. Becker, "A theory of social interactions," *Journal of Political Economy* 82 (1974), 1063–1093) and is compatible with the notion that "altruistic" behavior actually yields for the actor various psychological private goods including maintenance of self-esteem (R. F. Baumeister, "The self," in D. T. Gilbert, S. T. Fist and G. Lindzey (eds.) *The Handbook of Social Psychology*, 4th edn., vol. 1 (New York: McGraw-Hill, 1998)) and/or empathy (J. E. Batson, *The Altruism Question: Toward a Social-psychological Answer* (Hillsdale: Erlbaum, 1991); G. Clore and A. Ortney, "Cognition in emotion: Always, sometimes, never?" in R. D. Lane and L. Nadel (eds.), *Cognitive Neuroscience of Emotions* (Oxford: Oxford University Press, 2000), pp. 24–61; N. Eisenberg and R. A. Fabes, "Personality and socialization correlates of vicarious emotional responding," *Journal of*

Personality and Social Psychology 61 (3) (1991), 459) a sense of purpose, moral indignation, a sense of duty, guilt avoidance and desire for social approval. Some set of these psychological drivers likely underlies and contributes to ideological fervor.

12 H. Tajfel and J. C. Turner, "An integrative theory of intergroup conflict," in S. Worchel and W. G. Austin (eds.), *The Social Psychology of Intergroup Relations* (Monterey: Brooks/Cole, 1979).

13 T. I. Rowley and M. Moldoveanu, "When will stakeholder groups act? An interest- and identity-based model of stakeholder group mobilization," *Academy of Management Review* 28 (2) (2003), 204.

14 B. Klandersmans, "Social-psychological expansion of resource-mobilization theory," *American Sociological Review* 49 (1984), 583–600.

15 B. E. Ashforth, "'How can you do it?' Dirty work and the challenge of constructing a positive identity," *Academy of Management Review* 24 (3) (1999), 413; B. E. Ashforth, "Social identity theory and the organization," *Academy of Management Review* 14 (1) (1989), 20.

16 J. G. March and H. A. Simon, *Organizations* (New York: John Wiley & Sons, 1958).

17 Pfeffer and Salancik, *The External Control*.

18 Yaziji, "Turning gadflies," 110–115, for example.

19 www.nader.org/history/bollier_section_1.html, September 30, 2003.

6 | NGO *campaign types and company responses*

As indicated in the prior chapters, firms are increasingly facing campaigns by NGOs over a broad range of issues such as the environment, labor, human rights, consumer rights and animal rights. These campaigns are not all of a single kind; in fact, the campaigns come in two directly converse flavors. In this chapter we will differentiate between two very different types of campaigns – watchdog campaigns and proxy war campaigns (introduced in Chapter 1) – which need to be understood and responded to in very different ways.[1]

As mentioned in Chapter 4, early neo-institutional theory focused on how organizations, in order to gain and maintain the legitimacy necessary to survive, conform to institutional demands in the form of norms and rules.[2] While institutions are broad and often diffuse, institutional pressure must ultimately be brought to bear on organizations by other organizations that give expression to institutional norms. These "institutionally expressive" organizations might be governmental bodies, professional associations or nongovernmental watchdog or advocacy groups. In its most elementary structural form, a single institutionally expressive organization puts "institutional pressure" on a single organization. For example, a regulatory body may threaten to or actually fine a firm for failing to meet federal environmental guidelines.

In some cases, this pressure is applied blindly or "impersonally," meaning without regard to differences in institutionally neutral attributes of the organization or characteristics that are deemed irrelevant to the salient institutional issue. For example, only hospitals that meet a certain explicit set of requirements will be granted accreditation by a given accrediting agency.

In other cases, however, the institutional pressure is applied strategically. As discussed in the previous chapter, this is the case in NGO campaigns against corporations. The NGO behind the institutional pressure will apply pressure strategically, carefully choosing the target and tactics that it will employ depending on the goals it is trying to achieve.[3]

The advocacy organizations that carry out these campaigns are institutionally proactive in that they either hold firms accountable to dominant institutional norms, or they pursue institutional change through their campaigns against firms. Critically, these two categories of campaigns – holding firms accountable to dominant institutional norms and pursuing institutional change – are fundamentally different. These two different types of campaigns – "watchdog" and "proxy war" campaigns – have different goals, often select their targets differently, use different kinds of rhetoric with different audiences and use different kinds of tactics. In the sections that follow, we will highlight the differences between these two types of campaigns along these dimensions.[4]

Watchdog campaigns

A watchdog campaign, introduced in Section I, is one in which the goal is to pressure the targeted firm to comply with dominant institution standards. These standards may or may not be formalized in regulation. Watchdog campaigns are often run by local organizations that are responding to a perceived threat or harm to their local interests. An example of such campaigns would be a local NGO campaigning against a firm for its local impact, such as polluting a local river in violation of existing normative or regulative standards. These campaigns fit within the category of "isomorphic pressure" described by early neo-institutional scholars, as discussed in Chapter 4.[5]

Watchdog target selection

NGOs engaged in watchdog campaigns select their target firms most commonly because (1) the NGO perceives the firm to be infringing upon local interests through its specific actions and (2) there is a plausible story to be told about how these activities are in violation of accepted regulatory or social standards.

Watchdog rhetoric and audience

NGOs running watchdog campaigns accept and draw on the dominant institutions, in terms of both the content of the rhetoric and the key audiences. The demands that the NGOs make in these campaigns are not to change the institutional standards, but merely to better enforce them; the message is institutionally conservative. The campaigning NGO has the potential to appeal to a wide audience since it is drawing on broadly accepted norms including judicial, legislative and regulatory bodies.

In the case of isomorphic pressure campaigns, the rhetoric and framing of the complaint against the targeted organization is often in terms of the specific violations of existing standards by the targeted organization. Whether the institutional standards are formalized in regulation or not, these standards will be invoked as the appropriate measure by which the activity of the firm can be judged. In cases in which formal regulatory standards are present, the existing regulatory standards are assumed to be the appropriate basis of evaluation. The campaigning NGO will make claims to the effect that the targeted firm is in violation of these regulations.

In cases where there are no specific regulatory standards related to the activity of the firm, terms such as "accepted community standards" will be invoked. An example of this would be a campaign against a firm for its perceived "tasteless advertising." In such a case, the campaigning organization may recognize that regulation is impossible or unnecessary. The rhetoric will focus on demands for the firm to change its advertising practices, and claims will be made to the effect that the advertising is in violation of what is considered decent by the community.

With respect to targeted audiences in isomorphic campaigns, we would expect – in cases where there are formal enforcement systems – that regulators and other enforcement agencies and professional associations would be key audiences for the campaign. In the "purest" watchdog campaigns, courts would be used in cases where the issue is a "question of fact" rather than a "question of law." That is, a campaigning organization may use the courts to enforce the particular regulatory requirements, e.g. to get a court injunction for a particular type of behavior or to fine the targeted organization. They would not need to argue that the laws need further refinement, only that the facts of the case fall under the purview of a given law.

In cases where there are informal enforcement mechanisms, we would expect the campaigning organization to target its rhetoric to both members of the firm – to tap into their sense of shame – and broader society and other stakeholders that can apply pressure on the firm through social shame or withholding of resources. For instance, in the "tasteless advertising" example above, the owner may be shamed into complying with demands and third-party stakeholders, such as banks, may be more hesitant to do business with the offending firm.

Watchdog tactics

Tactics can be described by the degree to which watchdog NGOs use existing political, legal and regulatory institutions to attain the ends sought, and by how broadly accepted they are within the community at large. We have identified three different categories of tactics:

1. Lawsuits, lobbying of regulators and lobbying of politicians are tactics which can be described as "highly institutional."
2. Press conferences, rallies and marches might be considered "institutionally neutral" in that they rely less on political, legal and regulatory institutions, but do not contravene these institutions.
3. Civil disobedience, direct action to disrupt businesses and streets, destruction of property and violence are all tactics which, generally being illegal, contravene institutions and can be labeled "contra-institutional."

The tactics employed in watchdog campaigns tend to be "highly institutional" and/or "institutionally neutral." Mainstream and moderate advocacy organizations will tend to have more access to, and reliance upon, the resources housed within the dominant institutional bodies. Furthermore, more radical tactics will be more likely to alienate the institutionally conservative audiences that the NGO is targeting and thus the NGO will be loath to employ legitimacy-threatening radical tactics. The tactics often draw on established sources of institutional power, which, after all, are institutionally aligned with the goals of the campaign. The tactics may include, for example, appeals to courts and regulatory bodies.

Each of these institution-dependent tactics has many variants. For example, another tactic used by watchdog NGOs to advance their agenda is shareholder activism. Watchdog NGOs may buy shares of corporations and use ownership to forward proxies and other resolutions to effect change. They often use their status to urge institutional shareholders such as large public employee pension and retirement funds to pressure changes in corporate governance and conduct. They also work with and through socially responsible investment funds, serving as advisors and experts on ethical and social responsibility screens used to determine the composition of such funds, and by drawing attention to shortcomings in the mechanisms used by such funds to choose and retain specific stocks within their portfolios.[6]

Proxy war campaigns

Proxy wars – a form of "social movement" campaign – are designed to challenge and change the institutional framework, whether in terms of the formal regulatory and legal systems or accepted social norms and values. As carriers of a challenging ideology, the social movement organizations behind a campaign often engage in institutional proxy campaigns in which opposing institutions generate a proxy conflict between organizations which strategically interact to promote, sustain or represent the opposing institutions.[7] In proxy war campaigns, the goals of the targeting organization are:

1. To extend the application of the campaigning organization's own "home" institutions (whether values or regulations) to a new context.
2. To delegitimize the competing institution.
3. To establish a meta-institutional rule that holds that the home institution dominates or takes precedence over the competing institution in cases where the two institutions are in apparent conflict. All proxy wars concern the truth, appropriateness, applicability and importance of the beliefs, norms and values in conflict.

While the campaign appears to the casual observer to be a conflict between two organizations, it is, at a deeper level, actually an expression of a broader conflict over norms, values and regulatory environments – in short, institutions. This is represented in Figure 6.1 below.

This framing can be generalized across many scenarios. A timely example concerns what Samuel Huntington calls a "clash of civilizations" which is reified through proxy wars between organizations such as al-Qaeda and the US intelligence and defense departments. Other examples include campaigns over free trade and globalization, and the civil rights group campaigns in the 1950s–1970s.[8]

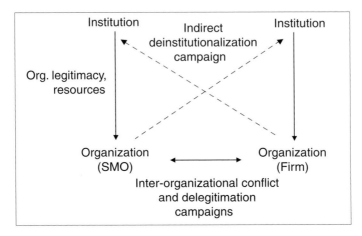

Figure 6.1 Institutional proxy wars

NGO campaigns against corporations are increasingly common. In these, the campaigning organization targets a given firm, but the goal is not simply to delegitimize the focal firm but rather to use it as an example of a dominant institution and to thereby show that the institution is problematic. Examples include:

- Campaigns against McDonald's as a representative organization of a larger institution, e.g. US multinational corporations.
- PETA campaigns against firms when the goal is actually a change of social norms and laws rather than just the change of a single firm's practices.
- Oxfam's campaign against GlaxoSmithKline, apparently concerning AIDS drugs in South Africa, but more fundamentally about the WTO's TRIPS agreement concerning intellectual property protection and the WTO itself.
- Other examples include campaigns against Nike's suppliers' labor practices in Southeast Asia, the catch methods of Starkist Tuna's suppliers and Monsanto's use of GMOs.

Proxy war target selection

In choosing which firm to target, NGOs take multiple factors into account, including prior public beliefs about the firm, how egregious the firm's behavior can be portrayed, the firm's willingness and ability to resist the campaign and how well it can be presented as exemplary or expressive of the institution that the NGO is attempting to undermine. This last basis of target selection merits further clarification.

First, firms are often targeted and face greater institutional pressure not because they fail to conform to dominant institutional standards – as is classically portrayed in most neo-institutional theory – but precisely because they do conform. In watchdog campaigns, the campaign is a form of institutional pressure to conform; in proxy wars, the campaign is a response to the firm's conforming to the "problematic" institution.

Second, they are targeted because they are exemplary representatives of an institution that is itself under challenge. For example, some anti-globalization protestors have disputed McDonald's corporate behaviors. They readily state that their main reason for choosing McDonald's as a target is because they take it to represent globalization and multinational corporations in general.

Proxy war rhetoric and audience

In proxy wars, the campaigning organization must put forward two different narratives – one that shows how egregious the focal firm is, and the other which highlights how this egregiousness is a natural outgrowth, expression or instantiation of a problematic institution. The tone and content of the rhetoric is often more ideologically radical than that of watchdog campaigns. The more fundamental the level of institutional change, the more radical the rhetoric tends to be. A more moderate campaign might call, for example, for a new system of carbon trading or a carbon tax, while a more radical campaign might call for nothing less than an immediate and complete end to the use of fossil fuels.

The degree of radicalism also affects which audience is targeted. In more moderate campaigns, key audiences will often be courts, regulators or legislators, since in this context these generally sympathetic groups often hold the power to quickly reshape regulatory institutions. Minor modifications in laws, their interpretation or their enforcement may be feasible through direct appeal to the various branches of government.

Where more radical change is desired, these audiences are less likely to be sympathetic, since they tend to reflect or be dependent upon the ideological status quo. Consequently, campaigns that are more radical often first attempt to appeal to the hearts and minds of the public at large or some more politically active segment of the population.

Proxy war tactics

Proxy war campaigns tend to rely on "institutionally neutral" and "contra-institutional" tactics, as discussed in Chapter 5. Contra-institutional tactics have a number of attributes that make them more attractive as an option for ideologically radical organizations than for more mainstream or moderate organizations. First, radical organizations, at odds with the dominant institutions, are less likely to have the resources and networks that are available to more mainstream or moderate organizations. This is somewhat due to a homogeneous group of resource providers, as opposed to the heterogeneous groupings other, more benign institutions would attract, as illustrated in Figure 6.2 below.

Second, positive feedback systems will tend to enforce this dynamic, as the use of radical tactics may tend to isolate the radical organization from more mainstream sources of capital as well as from key players in the dominant institutions. The mainstream holders of capital and individuals ensconced in institution networks have their own

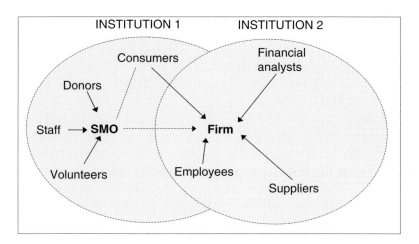

Figure 6.2 Institutional homogeneity and heterogeneity of resource providers

resource-dependencies – most likely on the dominant institutions – and will thus tend to avoid jeopardizing their own legitimacy within their field by providing support to radical organizations.

Third, radical organizations, being less reliant on dominant-institution resources, will be free to pursue these radical tactics. Likewise, by using contra-institutional tactics, radical organizations have already put themselves out of contention for access to resources tied to more ideologically mainstream resource providers. As a result, further use of radical tactics will not threaten the resources of the radical campaigning organization.

Finally, radical ideologies may justify and even demand radical tactics more easily than more moderate ideologies. For example, many of the members of PETA take seriously ethical theories that may *demand* radical tactics. Some are ethical utilitarians who believe that we must maximize the welfare of all *sentient beings* and that an animal's suffering is as morally significant as a human's welfare. Others are rights theorists who believe that if severely mentally handicapped humans have whatever attributes give them rights, then higher animals that share those capacities also have similar rights. Thus, from this perspective, animal "holocausts" are ongoing and whatever means necessary should be employed to stop them. Similarly, internally consistent reasoning may lead some pro-life groups to sanction, even if not publicly, violence against abortion practitioners.

Implications of campaigns for NGOs and corporations

In addition to being of theoretical interest, campaigns are of significant relevance as a tactic for NGOs as well as a potential risk for corporate managers. As noted in Chapter 4, the underlying drivers of these campaigns are mostly indicative of the continuing prominence of these campaigns. In this section we will consider the strengths and weaknesses of NGOs and corporations in the context of potential conflicting campaigns and discuss various approaches and tactics that both sides are likely to use with greater or lesser effectiveness.

Implications for NGOs

NGOs that attack firms have a number of advantages that make them especially effective. First, as highlighted in the section above, the advantage of univocality and institutionally homogeneous resource pools puts a wider choice of tactics at the disposal of NGOs embarking on a proxy war campaign. As we will see in Chapter 7, the more ideologically radical the NGO, the more homogeneity it is likely to have and the greater freedom it will have in terms of the tactics at its disposal.

At its most extreme, we see that perhaps the most influential NGO on the planet today, al-Qaeda, is highly influential at least in part because it is able to use very dramatic tactics in its campaign. It can use tactics that its adversaries are not able to use at least in part because of the broader range of stakeholders that they depend upon. This is equally, if less dramatically, true for NGOs campaigning against corporations. For example, the publicity stunts used by Greenpeace cannot be equally used by the targets of Greenpeace.

The disadvantage of the radicalism that generates this freedom in terms of tactics is that radicalism means that most of the society is not initially in agreement with the NGO's ideology. This does not get in the way of campaigns intended to simply raise awareness, nor does it get in the way of campaigns targeting a very narrow sympathetic audience. However, it will make the job of the NGO harder if the goal of the campaign requires convincing an ideologically mainstream audience of the legitimacy of the NGO's goals. Exacerbating this problem is the potential of more radical tactics to themselves alienate audience members.

Second, NGOs have, as an "industry," much greater legitimacy than firms. Figure 6.3 summarizes the results of a World Economic Forum survey in which citizens were asked to indicate which institutions and leaders they most trusted. Figures 6.4 and 6.5 present results of a similar survey by Edelman Public Relations of European citizens. Together, these data suggest that NGOs and their leaders are consistently trusted more than firms, and often more than governments and international organizations.

NGOs are often seen as working in the public interest, at least as construed by the NGO itself. By contrast, corporations are seen as being driven primarily by shareholder interest or the profit motive. The result is that NGOs are more likely to be assumed to be working in the interests of the audience of a campaign. Furthermore, the statements made by NGOs are more likely to be seen as unbiased by a profit motive. Smart NGOs will leverage this legitimacy advantage

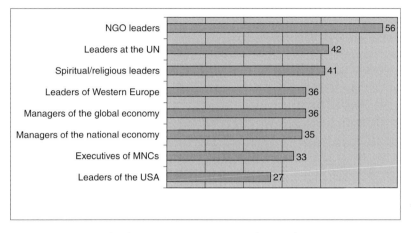

Figure 6.3 Trust in leaders: percentage saying "a lot" and "some trust" (average across all fifteen countries surveyed).
Source: World Economic Forum (www.weforum.org)

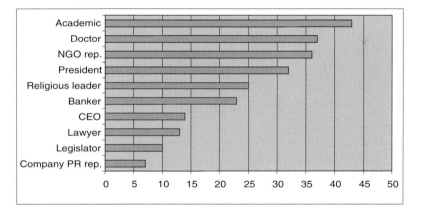

Figure 6.4 Credibility of spokespersons, USA, percentage of "thought leader" respondents who give "very high" or "high" credibility to the spokespersons.
Source: Edelman Trust Barometer 2003 (www.edelman.co.uk/trustbarometer)

through such actions as highlighting its own mission or its donor base, while accentuating the profit-motive of the targeted firm through such tactics as pulling "illustrative" statements made by representatives of the corporation. These statements are usually easy to find among CEO statements to financial analysts.

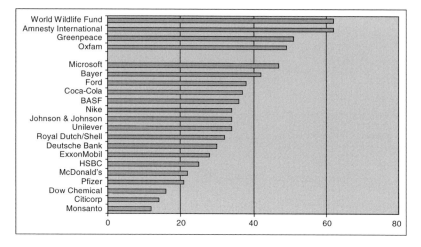

Figure 6.5 European trust in brands, percentage of "thought leader" respondents who trust the brand "very highly" or "highly".
Source: Edelman Trust Barometer 2008 (www.edelman.co.uk/trustbarometer)

Third, in addition to their greater legitimacy, NGOs are also regularly seen as underdogs, which can bring audience sympathy. Corporations are seen as mighty beasts whereas NGOs often portray themselves as much smaller players with much less resources at their disposal. Of course, the downside for NGOs is that they often are in fact at a major resource disadvantage compared to corporations. A related disadvantage for NGOs is that members of the public might have various other stereotypes about NGOs (e.g., "damn hippies," "idealists," "naïve," "extremists") or may simply be a little less comfortable about NGOs because they might be less familiar, as a category, than corporations.

Fourth, NGOs, while being resource poor, tend to cooperate more with one another than firms do, and thus when an NGO "industry" goes up against a market industry, it has a competitive advantage. Being on the attack, it is often easier to bring in additional NGOs to support a campaign. Interestingly, the more effective the campaign is perceived to be, the easier it is to bring in many additional NGOs, who are keen to be associated with a winning effort. By contrast, if a firm is under attack, it will tend to have a harder time to bring in public support from other corporations. First, other corporations are normally competing against the targeted firm and thus have less of a tendency to cooperate in the context of a campaign. Additionally, to publicly support a competitor who is under attack will increase the probability of one's own firm to be targeted as well.

Fifth, NGOs are designed around and focused on their causes, whereas firms are primarily focused on and designed to optimize their market performance. Thus, while firms are, at root, economic agents, NGOs are social and political agents. As a result, NGOs tend to be good at social and political maneuvering, whereas firms are often more maladroit.

Corporate managers are generally focused on key variables of competition such as product characteristics and price. However, the issues that concern NGOs are often different, and thus managers tend to be less cognizant of these issues. Campaigns are often over production processes such as the labor practices, the worthiness of the product itself (e.g. protesters are not complaining about furs not being soft enough or cigarettes not being tasty enough) and negative input and output externalities such as the opportunity costs of the clear-cutting of forests or the costs incurred by third parties as a result of pollution. Recognizing the broader range of potential issues is the first step toward dealing with social risk.

Additionally, in market competition, it is usually "every firm for itself" in a contest for market share and profits. By contrast, NGOs, being relatively resource-poor and often sharing similar social, political and economic goals, tend to join in coalitions or "swarms" to attack a particular targeted firm through myriad tactics. Yaziji found coalitions of 200 or more NGOs in a single campaign to be common.[9]

Also, as dedicated political and social players, NGOs do not need to balance their goals or campaign resources against some other organizational imperative such as maximizing economic performance to the same extent as firms do. Although targeted firms often have tremendous resources, most of them are dedicated to goals of market competition and are thus unavailable for responding to NGO campaigns.

Finally, another source of effectiveness of NGOs in their campaigns is that they are the initiators and on the offense. This means that they get to choose their *targets, tactics, timing* and *framing* of issues to optimize their impact. The importance of this is difficult to overstate. Effective campaigning NGOs will pick targets that are especially vulnerable. In Chapter 4 we highlighted some of the risk factors for firms. Smart NGOs will pick their targets carefully according to the firm's vulnerabilities.

With regard to tactics, NGOs will often have a careful balancing act in terms of the tactics that they use. More radical tactics will tend to generate more publicity, but this may be at the expense of alienating some of the audience. Think again of al-Qaeda's tactics, the graphic advertisements of PETA or the exhumation of relatives of a company's CEO by Stop Huntington Animal Cruelty (SHAC). These campaigns grab headlines but might be found distasteful by some.

Smart NGOs will think carefully about the goals of their campaign. Some campaigns are designed more to raise the prominence of an issue in general, rather than to win, for example, passage of a particular piece of legislation. In such consciousness-raising campaigns, radical tactics might be optimal as they do indeed shock and raise awareness of an issue. For example, the radical tactics by the small NGO SHAC have been incredibly effective in bringing attention to animal rights issues.

Smart NGOs need to also ensure that their tactics are aligned with the expectations of their supporters. For example, more ideologically mainstream NGOs will not be able to use radical tactics without alienating their more mainstream supporters. These NGOs will tend to use more mainstream tactics which are less alienating and which are more likely to be seen as reasonable by a larger portion of the population.

NGOs may often work more or less in collaboration with other NGOs, with a joint "good cop, bad cop" strategy, with more radical NGOs raising the issue through radical tactics, while a more moderate NGO provides a "compromise" alternative to the targeted firm.

Another dimension of the goal of the campaign that is relevant is how the campaign fits into a broader longer-term strategy. For example, PETA decided to change the practices of the fast-food industry, at a firm-by-firm level, but using powerful spillover effects across campaigns. It routinely puts forward a relatively low-publicity set of demands to a fast-food firm and threatens a campaign if the demands are not met. If a firm decides not to meet these demands, PETA runs a very high profile campaign until the firm meets its demands. PETA then moves on to a second firm in the industry with another set of demands. Often this second firm, having seen the bad press of the first campaign, meets the demands rather than facing a campaign against it. Then PETA moves on to the next firm. This is covered in greater detail in the PETA case illustration following this chapter.

With regard to timing, campaigning NGOs can choose when to launch an attack. This choice will often be driven by the NGO's own preparedness for the campaign, together with co-campaigning partner NGOs, but may be affected or even driven by particular events in the outside environment. For example, if there is a major environmental disaster, a critical piece of legislation is being debated or a firm is making a large strategic investment decision, the NGOs may need to modify its campaign calendar. Aptly prepared NGOs have their long-term strategies and plans and build their resources and plan their activities accordingly, but will be responsive to the changing environment and modify their strategies to some extent based on this changing environment.

Additionally, NGOs are often value-driven organizations, with volunteers or paid staff that are highly dedicated to and passionate about the goals of their organization. This increases the effectiveness of the NGO relative to its size.

Finally, an NGO launching a campaign has the advantage of being the first to frame the issues; and, as any expert in rhetoric or public relations knows, the original framing of an issue can heavily influence the debate that follows. The NGOs that campaigned against pharmaceutical firms for their pricing and patent protection for AIDS drugs in South Africa defined the issue as "people versus profits." The pharmaceutical companies, such as GlaxoSmithKline, tried unsuccessfully to redefine the debate as one of protecting lives through innovation and patents. In addition, as discussed in Chapter 3, there are multiple levels of ethical claims that can be used by an NGO in its campaign. NGOs will pick the angles that most effectively advance their cause and will invest heavily upfront to lock in the terms of the debate moving forward.

Implications for companies and their managers

While specific prescriptions are beyond the scope of this chapter, the foregoing discussion of the phenomenon of social risk does suggest some general approaches to the strategic management of social risk.

Through our qualitative research, some "best practices" for managing social risk and campaigns have become apparent. We will divide the suggestions into two categories: (1) avoiding attacks and (2) responding to attacks. Perhaps the first point is that many of the variables affecting social risk can only marginally be considered choice variables since existing firms have limited flexibility in choosing, for example, the social, economic or institutional environment in which they operate.

For some other variables which are choice variables for the firm, such as how well known it is, other considerations – such as the value of the brand to market performance – will tend to dominate any social risk considerations. For instance, it is not strategically smart for McDonald's to incur all the losses that would go along with a smaller brand in order to reduce its social risk exposure. In analyzing the construct of social risk, we identified three key sub-dimensions: size, probability and uncertainty. The intensity and form of social risk management will depend on all three of these dimensions as well as on timeframes. For instance, at one end of the continuum, a firm might face a small magnitude, low probability risk that is practically impossible to track and prevent. Such a risk might best be ignored. At the other end of the continuum, a discrete, substantive, current social risk that the firm has some ability to learn about should likely minimally generate efforts to gather information and make a decision regarding the best proactive or reactive strategies. A full accounting of social risk management must, therefore, give due consideration to the role of uncertainty. Given this, one of the key aspects of managing social risk will be to identify and reduce uncertainty where possible and cost-effective, i.e., where there is an optimal trade-off among risk-avoidance opportunity costs, risk-management costs and risk-loss costs.

Managers should understand social risk as a continuously evolving phenomenon, not a static characteristic of the environment. Thus, environmental sensing and interpreting will likely be critical social risk management activities to minimize state, effect and response uncertainty.[10]

The approach to the management of social risk should likely also be holistic and focused on trends, in recognition of the high level of interrelatedness and co-evolution of the variables and players involved. An approach that just focuses on perceived key actors or specific challenges is unlikely to provide as much foresight as an approach based at least partially on trend-watching and dynamics-tracking.

In avoiding attacks, the first steps are to identify and minimize exposure. Thus, managers should consider what risk factors their firms face, as discussed above. Also, firms must remain cognizant of the distinction between what is legal and what is legitimate. NGOs engaged in efforts to change industry-wide practices, laws or institutions often attack firms regardless of whether the firm is law-abiding.

Firms should also try to map out the relevant NGOs. These include radical organizations that could only be considered as potential threats as well as less radical organizations, which might be partners rather than attackers. Pre-emptive engagement with NGOs can provide a wide range of benefits in reducing the downside of social risk and increasing the upside.[11]

Managers should keep in mind the relative lack of trustworthiness or credibility that most firms have. If a more legitimate NGO makes claims against a less legitimate firm whose motives in defending itself are immediately suspect, firms begin at a basic disadvantage in the court of public opinion. Building legitimacy and trust as a good corporate citizen should be an ongoing effort.

Suchman strategies

Responses to campaigns invariably include a component of maintaining or regaining legitimacy. Suchman identified generic strategies (compromise, ignore, defend, counter-attack) for doing so. However, two complications are worth discussing.[12]

Suchman assumed that the loss of legitimacy was the result of failing to meet existing dominant institutional standards. But since campaigns are often launched as a form of proxy war, closer hewing to the dominant standards is unlikely to satisfy the campaigning organizations. Firms under attack need to determine the goal of the attack: is it to change the firm's behavior (as in a watchdog campaign), or to change the rules of the game (as in a proxy war campaign)? The optimal response could well depend on the goals of the attacking NGOs.

Additionally, the short-, medium- and long-term consequences must be taken into account. Some firms negotiate and make concessions as soon as they are challenged. This may relieve the immediate pressure but invite further attacks. So, seen from the medium term, making concessions might seem like a bad idea. But in the long term, reputations and relationships matter and having a good reputation and having positive ongoing relationships with all the stakeholders that can affect the firm greatly reduces the firm's social risk.

This reasoning only captures a partial truth and actually confuses the medium term with the long term. For very high profile organizations, it is likely that evaluation and critiques should best be taken as a permanent condition. Given this, close and ongoing cooperation and communication and compromise with relevant NGOs might actually be the optimal long-term approach. Earning a good reputation and the trust of NGOs might be difficult and costly over the medium term, but beneficial over the long term.

Conclusion

This chapter has defined social risk in terms of potential downside – as is the want of most strategy scholars and managers. This is a simplifying, but inaccurate, assumption. There are good reasons to believe that an environment that generates risk of normative delegitimation for firms can be a source of competitive advantage for firms that are well adapted to it, relative to their competitors. For example, firms that respond as first-movers to shifts in the social environment and to social risk may outperform firms that do not because they may gain leads in innovation, meet latent demand, have better brand image and be better able to meet future regulatory demands at a lower cost.

This chapter has built upon our discussion of NGO tactics, strategies, targets and timing of attacks by further exploring watchdog and proxy war subdivisions. The negative impact that some NGOs have on firms are insurmountable when firms decide to ignore warning signs or do not adequately respond to NGO considerations. Ideally, firms will be aware of potential attacks from NGOs, however, this is nearly impossible to predict. The best response seems to be deterring relationships laden with animosity, and instead refocusing on some level of collaboration between the firm and NGO.

In the next chapter, we will turn our attention from the conflictual relationships between NGOs and corporations to the various forms of collaboration between players from the two sectors. These collaborative relationships are blossoming in many different forms, presenting exciting benefits for NGOs and corporations, as well as often a broader set of stakeholders.

Notes

1 The discussion presented in this chapter draws on three years of qualitative research including interviews, case studies and a large-scale global survey of NGOs that have campaigned against firms. For more detailed information on the research results and research methods, see M. Yaziji, "Institutional change and social risk: A study of campaigns by social movement organizations against firms," INSEAD (2004).

2 P. J. DiMaggio and W. W. Powell, "The iron cage revisited: Institutional isomorphism and collective rationality in organizational fields," *American Sociological Review* 48 (1983), 147–160; J. W. Meyer and B. Rowan, "Institutionalized organizations: Formal structure as myth and ceremony," *American Journal of Sociology* 83 (1977), 340–363.

3 F. Den Hond and F. G. A. De Bakker, "Ideologically motivated activism: How activist groups influence corporate social change activities," *Academy of Management Review* 32 (4) (2007), 1292–1295.

4 These two sorts of campaigns are "ideal types" and in reality there is a continuum between the two. Nonetheless, as we shall see, there are some important qualitative differences between the two that need to be appreciated for practical as well as theoretical reasons.

5 DiMaggio and Powell, "The iron cage"; Meyer and Rowan, "Institutionalized organizations."

6 T. Guay, J. P. Doh and G. Sinclair, "Nongovernmental organizations, shareholder activism and socially responsible investments: Ethical, strategic and governance implications," *Journal of Business Ethics* 52 (1) (2004), 125–139.

7 NGO is a term of art and can include anything from church groups to chess clubs to watchdog groups to radical social movement organizations bent on the destruction of the status quo. Social movement organizations pursue institutional change, from moderate to radical.

8 S. P. Huntington, *The Clash of Civilizations and the Remaking of World Order* (New York: Simon & Schuster, 1996).

9 Yaziji, "Institutional change."

10 F. J. Milliken, "Three types of perceived uncertainty about the environment: State, effect, and response uncertainty," *Academy of Management Review* 12 (1) (1987), 133.

11 Yaziji, "Institutional change."

12 M. C. Suchman, "Managing legitimacy: Strategic and institutional approaches," *Academy of Management Review* 20 (3) (1995), 571–610.

Case illustration: PETA and KFC

People for the Ethical Treatment of Animals (PETA) is one of the world's most effective advocacy NGOs. With over 750,000 members spanning the globe, PETA has led successful campaigns against McDonald's, Wendy's and Burger King. McDonald's agreed to sweeping animal welfare improvements after PETA pressured them for almost a year with over 400 demonstrations across the globe, celebrity endorsements and advertisements. Burger King was next on PETA's menu, and the company made concessions after only six months and around 800 protests. Wendy's followed suit in September 2001. Dan Shannon, PETA's Vegan Outreach Coordinator, believes, "Companies are waking up to the fact that consumers care about these issues. Our campaigns impact adversely on their sales figures and their stock prices and so force them to make changes."[1] KFC, however, has proven a formidable opponent to PETA's tactics and has not conceded as readily as other fast-food restaurants facing PETA pressure.

KFC, which is owned by Yum! Brands, is the largest retailer of chicken in the world. While Yum! Brands does not raise chickens, the company recognizes their responsibility to influence how animals are treated by their suppliers. KFC's Animal Welfare Program website states that, "Our goal is to only deal with suppliers who provide an environment that is free from cruelty, abuse and neglect."[2] Based on KFC's assertions to "raise the bar" in animal welfare, PETA agreed to work with the company in 2001. From April 2001 until January 2003, PETA and KFC attempted to collaborate. On April 25, 2001, PETA wrote to KFC complaining of animal cruelty, which kicked off two years of negotiations between the groups. KFC pledged to improve chicken welfare and had created the KFC Animal Welfare Advisory Council in late 2000, hiring four of five PETA-endorsed scientists. PETA spent two years trying to convince KFC that its suppliers do not treat chickens humanely. Some of PETA's chief concerns included breeding programs that created chickens with upper bodies too large

112

to be supported by their legs, infrequent litter changing, mutilation, food and water deprivation and inhumane slaughter techniques.[3] According to PETA's Director of Vegan Outreach, Bruce Friedrich, in the two years of working together, KFC audited its slaughterhouses for gratuitous cruelty, which did result in some improvement. However, the improvements were not enough.[4] The two organizations lacked shared goals and did not agree on what constituted "animal welfare." Communication breakdown led to the meltdown of the attempted collaboration.

In January 2003, PETA determined that KFC did not intend to improve animal welfare to PETA's standards and launched a negative campaign and boycott against the company. PETA enlisted a number of celebrities to join its campaign, including Pamela Anderson, the Dalai Lama and Paul McCartney. PETA has staged thousands of protests and demonstrations around the world against KFC, sometimes in the hometowns of executives. In Germany, a PETA member drenched Yum! Brands CEO David Novak with fake blood, a photograph proudly displayed on the PETA-sponsored "KentuckyFriedCruelty" website.[5] PETA has also filed lawsuits against KFC and heavily promoted an undercover investigation of its source farms.

PETA has not wavered in its worldwide KFC ban. During 2006 alone, protests outside of KFC outlets and proposed future KFC stores have consisted of messages ranging from suppliers' cruelty to animals to illegal transporting of animals.[6] Activists carried signs and "imprisoned" themselves as a way to symbolize the cruelty and hardships chickens on KFC supply farms endure. Despite all the efforts, KFC still maintains its position not only in the market, but in its belief that the company and suppliers act within acceptable humane boundaries.

What began as collaboration between a corporation and an NGO evolved into hostility. KFC did make changes while working with PETA, but not enough to satisfy the NGO. Corporate–NGO collaborations can reach a breaking point when one simply acts to "appease" the other, as seemed to be the case with KFC and PETA. Whether KFC agreed to make changes simply to deter future focus on the company is unknown. If that in fact was one of the motivators, PETA responded with great fervor, using KFC as a springboard to show other corporations that extreme, if not complete collaboration will need to take place in order for certain NGOs to step down. Otherwise, making half-concerted efforts towards certain expectations, visions and standards will simply fuel the fire.

Notes

1 A. Blyth, "KFC and PETA," *Ethical Corporation* July 26 (2003), available at www.ethicalcorp.com/content.asp?ContentID=854. Accessed December 5, 2005.
2 KFC, "Animal Welfare Program" (2005), available at www.kfc.com/responsibility/animalwelfare_progress.htm. Accessed December 6, 2005.
3 Blyth, "KFC and PETA."
4 Blyth, "KFC and PETA."
5 Kentucky Fried Cruelty, "Campaign Highlights" (2005), available at www.kentuckyfriedcruelty.com/highlights.asp. Accessed December 6, 2005.
6 "PETA plans protest outside KFC outlet," *The Hindu* August 11 (2006), available at www.hindu.com/2006/08/11/stories/2006081119461300.htm. Accessed December 23, 2007.

Case illustration: Coca-Cola in India

Coca-Cola is a virtually omnipresent product, and as such has endured its fair share of both acceptance and resistance. In one instance, Coca-Cola was the target of a snowballing global campaign by NGOs that has cost the company millions of dollars. While Coke has tried to collaborate with certain environmental NGOs, the company is still mainly involved in conflictual corporate–NGO relationships.

Coke has had particular trouble in India, where it has been accused of creating water shortages, polluting groundwater and soil, and exposing its customers to toxic waste and pesticides. Activist Amit Srivastava, who runs a California-based NGO known as Global Resistance, toured American college campuses in 2005 spreading the message that, "[Coke] is destroying lives, it is destroying livelihoods and it is destroying communities all across India." Srivastava is rallying American and European college students against Coca-Cola. In response, colleges such as Bard College in New York, Carleton College in Minnesota and Oberlin College in Ohio have banned Coke products on campus. Srivastava's website, www.indiaresource.org, is a global stage and means of communication for activists and pro-testers, drawing about 20,000 visitors a month. On the other hand, www.cokefacts.org, designed by Coke to counter NGO allegations, only draws 800 visitors a month.[1] Coca-Cola has been struggling against a number of global, activist NGOs to protect its reputation.

In India, the company has been compelled to contest a number of legal battles. For instance, in the state of Rajasthan, Coke had to fight a court order requiring it to list pesticide residues on its labels. Coke claims the levels are safe, but tests from the Center for Science and Environment (CSE), a New Delhi-based NGO, claim otherwise. The CSE found that Coke, along with other soft drinks manufactured in the area, contained residues of four extremely toxic pesticides and insecticides – lindane, DDT, malathion and chlorpyrifos. According to Sunita Narain, director of CSE, "In all the samples tested, the levels of pesticide residue far exceeded the maximum permissible total pesticide limit of 0.0005 mg per liter in water used as food, set down by the European Economic Commission (EEC)."[2] According to CSE, the pesticides could cause long-term cancer, damage to the nervous and reproductive systems, birth defects and severe disruption of the immune system. In response, Sanjeev Gupta, president of Coca-Cola India, called CSE's claims "unfair" and portrayed Coke's situation as a "trial by media."[3]

Coke has further fielded criticism about its effects on water levels in India. In 2004, the Central Ground Water Board found that a Coca-Cola bottling plant in Kaladera, India, was responsible for the decline in the groundwater table in the area. The factory was found to be taking out massive amounts of water and causing ecological imbalance in the region by disturbing the deeper aquifers through its heavy-duty bore wells. The Board's investigation was the result of a directive by the Consultative Committee of the Union Ministry of Water Resources. Residents of Kaladera demanded the plant's permanent closure, which they blame for scarcity of water in as many as fifty villages. Activists from Gandhian and Sarvodaya bodies to the Shiv Sena have taken up the cause, helping to organize a bandh in Kaladera and a huge public meeting to demand the plant's closure. The Sangharsh Samiti (struggle committee) intensified its campaign with the slogan "Coca-Cola bhagao, paani bachao," which translates to "Drive away Coca-Cola, save the water."[4] In the southern state of Kerala in March 2004, local officials shut down a $16 million Coke bottling plant after similar allegations that it drained and polluted local water.[5] In Coca-Cola's defense, water continued to dry up even after the factory closed, and lack of rainfall was more significant than the plant's presence. NGOs still do not think that Coke should be located in areas where drought is an issue.[6]

In the opinion of David Cox, the Hong Kong-based communications director for Asia Coke, Mr. Srivastava and other activists "are making false environmental allegations against us to further an anti-globalization agenda."[7] Sometimes the NGOs admit to using false claims. For example, Srivastava admits that in 2004, NGOs spread stories of Indian farmers using Coke on their crops as pesticide mainly as a publicity stunt.[8] According to the www.cokefacts.org website, Coke is now working with the Central Ground Water Authority and NGOs in India to harvest rainwater to restore groundwater tables.[9]

Coca-Cola India even collaborated with Delhi-based NGO FORCE to organize a seminar to educate others about how important it is to harvest rainwater in India.

Coca-Cola has recently employed The Energy and Resources Institute (TERI) to assess its operations in India. These investigations have been conducted based on claims that Coca-Cola has engaged in unethical production practices in India. These alleged practices include causing severe water shortages, locating water-extracting plants in "drought prone" areas, further limiting water access by contaminating the surrounding land and groundwater, and irresponsibly disposing of toxic waste. These practices make it extremely difficult for India's residents to meet basic daily water requirements. Colleges and universities throughout the US, UK and Canada have joined in holding the company accountable for its overseas business practices by banning Coca-Cola products on their campuses until more positive results are reported. However, critics argue that TERI's assessment will undoubtedly be biased since the organization has been largely funded by The Coca-Cola Company.[10]

Coca-Cola stands behind the safety of its products. "Multinational corporations provide an easy target," says Amulya Ganguli, a political analyst in New Delhi. "These corporations are believed to be greedy, devoted solely to profit, and uncaring about the health of the consumers." There is also a deeply rooted distrust of big business and particularly foreign big business in India.[11] This is a reminder that there will continue to be obstacles, as there were in the past, to foreign investments in India. In order to reaffirm their presence in India, Coke and Pepsi have run separate ads insisting that their drinks are safe. Coke's ad said "Is there anything safer for you to drink?" and invited Indians to visit its plants to see how the beverage is made.[12] Nevertheless, in July 2006, Coke reported a 12 percent decline in sales.[13]

Coca-Cola has taken various initiatives to improve the drinking water conditions for those around the world. It has formally pledged support for the United Nations Global Compact and co-founded the Global Water Challenge, which improves water access and sanitation in countries in critical need. It is improving energy and efficiency through the use of hydrofluorocarbon-free insulation for 98 percent of new refrigeration sales and marketing equipment.

Specifically in India, Coke has stated that "More than 1/3 of the total water that is used in operations is renewed and returned to groundwater systems."[14] Coca-Cola is installing 270 devices to catch rainwater, and plans to install fifty more water-catching devices in 2008. The company will also be distributing a kit that works to improve the water-use efficiency of its bottlers.[15] Inspecting its own water use habits, Coca-Cola has vowed to reduce the amount of water it uses in its bottling operations. As of June 2007, Coca-Cola had reduced the amount of water needed to make one liter of Coke to 2.54 liters (compared with 3.14 liters five years earlier).[16]

More broadly, Coke has sought to develop more comprehensive solutions to global water challenges, working with a leading environmental NGO. At the June 2007 annual meeting of the WWF in Beijing, Coca-Cola announced its multi-year partnership with the organization "to conserve and protect freshwater resources." E. Neville Isdell, Chairman and CEO of The Coca-Cola Company, said, "Our goal is to replace every drop of water we use in our beverages and their production. For us that means reducing the amount of water used to produce our beverages, recycling water used for manufacturing processes so it can be returned safely to the environment, and replenishing water in communities and nature through locally relevant projects." Coca-Cola hopes to spread these practices to other members of its supply chain, particularly the sugar cane industry. The Coca-Cola–WWF partnership also focuses on climate protection and protection of seven of the world's "most critical freshwater basins," including the Yangtze in China. Although Coca-Cola's corporate social responsibility has included other projects with WWF in the past, it hopes that this official partnership will help achieve larger-scale results and ward off some of the negative reactions it has received to its operations in India and elsewhere.[17]

Notes

1 S. Stecklow, "How a global web of activists gives Coke problems in India," *Wall Street Journal* June 7 (2005), A1.
2 R. Devraj, "Indian Coke, Pepsi laced with pesticides, says NGO," available at www.indiaresource.org/news/2003/4725.html. Accessed November 22, 2005.
3 Devraj, "Indian Coke."
4 "Coca-Cola responsible for decline in groundwater table in Rajasthan," *The Hindu* (2004), available at www.indiaresource.org/news/2004/1020. html. Accessed November 22, 2005.

5 Stecklow, "How a global web," A1.

6 Stecklow, "How a global web," A1.

7 Stecklow, "How a global web," A1.

8 Stecklow, "How a global web," A1.

9 "Coke facts: India: Environmental initiatives" (2005), available at www.cokefacts.org/citizenship/cit_in_environmental.shtml. Accessed November 22, 2005.

10 Amit Srivastava, "Coca-Cola funded group investigates Coca-Cola in India," *India Resource Center* April 16 (2007), available at www. indiaresource.org/campaigns/coke/2007/coketeri.html.

11 Mark Sappenfield, "India's cola revolt taps into old distrust; behind contradictory reports of pesticides in Coke and Pepsi is an underlying wariness of foreign companies," *The Christian Science Monitor* September 1 (2006), available at www.monitorweek.net/2006/0901/p06s01-wosc.html.

12 Amelia Gentleman, "For 2 giants of soft drinks, a crisis in crucial market," *New York Times* August 23 (2006), C3.

13 P. Wonacott and C. Terhune, "Path to India's market dotted with potholes," *Wall Street Journal* September 12 (2006), available at http://online.wsj.com/article/SB115801500763459902.html?mod=seekingalpha.

14 "Coca-Cola-India: Key facts," available at www.cokefacts.org.

15 "Coca-Cola-India: Key facts."

16 Ben Blanchard, "Coke vows to reduce water used in drink production," June 5 (2007), available at www.reuters.com.

17 "The Coca-Cola Company pledges to replace the water it uses in its beverages and their production," *Press Release* June 5 (2007), available at www.thecoca-colacompany.com/presscenter/nr_20070605_tccc_and_wwf_partnership.html.

PART III

Corporate–NGO engagement

7 | Corporate–NGO engagements: from conflict to collaboration

Corporate–NGO engagement has gained increased attention in both academic and practitioner circles. As discussed in Section II of this book, some NGOs have explicitly targeted corporations, seeking to pressure companies and managers to assume greater responsibility for the negative spillovers of their actions. It is in this context that many corporations confront NGOs and undertake formal or informal relationships with organizations that may have targeted and continue to target these very same companies with campaigns.

Collaborations among corporations and NGOs are now so common that they are a growing subject of management research.[1] For NGOs, partnerships with corporations may yield financial, human resource and reputation benefits. For corporate partners, relationships with NGOs provide access to skills, competencies and capabilities that support their CSR efforts and are otherwise unavailable within their organizations or from alliances with for-profit firms. These "combinative" capabilities have the potential to provide both partners with discernable benefits.[2]

One challenge in reviewing the literature and contributions on corporate–NGO engagement, especially those involving collaborative or cooperative relations, is that "studies of CSSPs [cross sectoral social partnerships or corporate–NGO relationships] emerge from various disciplines such as organization studies, public policy and administration, economics, nonprofit management, health care, education and the natural environment."[3] In this chapter, we review this literature in order to frame the interactions that characterize corporate–NGO engagement. We introduce a number of typologies that have been used to classify the different types of corporate–NGO engagement, reflecting different levels of commitment and intensity in the relationship on the part of each party, and the different goals and purposes of these two organizational forms. We summarize recent research that describes the conditions under which corporate–NGO engagement can productively harness the resources of both participants, and where the "fit" between corporate and NGO resources and capabilities may be unproductive and efforts to collaborate unsuccessful. We describe the different resources and capabilities that both NGOs and corporations bring to the table and the types of collaborations that can help both the NGO and the firm achieve their respective goals. We will also discuss the unique challenges that face this particular form of inter-organizational collaboration.

Collaboration classifications and perspectives

Hess *et al.* report that "many of these new corporate social initiatives are taking on aspects more commonly associated with corporate strategy than community relations; they are grounded in the core competencies of the firm and related to the firm's long-term strategy."[4] As Selsky and Parker note in their review of literature on CSSPs,[5] the terminology for these relationships varies, and includes social partnerships,[6] intersectoral partnerships,[7] social alliances,[8] issues management alliances[9] and strategic partnerships.[10]

These connections can also be viewed through a range of frameworks and models. Selsky and Parker argue that there are two main "platforms" that have typified management and organization research on cross-sectoral partnerships: resource dependence and social issues.[11] They add a third platform, which they call the societal sector. As discussed in Chapter 2, these relationships can also be seen within the realm of network theory, an extension of the resource-dependency perspective. Alliances involve resource complementarities among firms,[12] some of which include social effects, such as legitimacy,[13] which appears to be a principal goal of corporations in their cooperative behavior with NGOs. Argenti, for example, details Starbucks' ongoing relationship with Conservation International and other NGOs.[14]

Austin describes the three stages in the "Collaborative Continuum" in the US as philanthropic, transactional and integrative.[15] The philanthropic stage is the most traditional and common relationship, where business generally makes a monetary donation to the nonprofit organization. The transactional stage includes specific activities and a two-way value exchange. The integrative stage is still small (but growing) and sees the collaboration combining values, missions and strategies. According to Austin, there is a significant shift among

Figure 7.1 Continuum of corporate–NGO engagement (adapted from Austin, *The Collaboration Challenge* and Lindenberg, "Reaching beyond the family")

businesses in the US to the transactional stage, with some evidence that corporations and NGOs are increasingly pursuing integrative relationships.[16] Building on Austin's typology, Lindenberg argues that nonprofit–business partnerships can be conceptualized along a continuum that includes: suspicion, interaction, philanthropy, transactional and integrative behavior (see Figure 7.1).[17]

Parker and Selsky examined the behavioral dynamics of cause-based partnerships (CBPs). They argue that the dynamics of these relationships can be best understood in terms of an emergent culture. They present three scenarios – integration, reculturation and separation – to illustrate how participants in CBPs continually negotiate a workable set of cultural practices among themselves. In their review of literature on corporate, not-for-profit and public sector relationships, Selsky and Parker suggest that project-based cross-sector partnerships to address social issues (CSSPs) occur in four "arenas": business–nonprofit, business–government, government–nonprofit and trisector.[18] They argue that, "Demands for corporate social responsibility encourage businesses to partner, nonprofits are motivated by demands for improved efficiency and accountability, and governments are encouraged to provide more benefits and services while being both less intrusive and more transparent."[19]

There is some evidence that direct and ongoing engagement with NGOs is more likely to occur in the more advanced stages of developing CSR policies and that companies in earlier stages are less equipped to take on the challenges associated with close collaborations.[20] Although there have been limited attempts to provide generic classifications of corporate approaches to these relationships, e.g. "proactive" versus "reactive,"[21] there have been few systematic efforts to locate these relationships within the broader relationships among stakeholders in business and society, with some exceptions.[22]

As discussed in Chapter 2, the role of NGOs in broader societies may be approached from the perspective of research on social networks and alliances. Similarly, dyadic business–NGO relationships may also be viewed from the perspective of social network and related theories.

Trust is a fundamental principle in social network theory and perspectives on social capital.[23] Research has shown the reciprocal effects of trust in alliance relationships, demonstrating that trust leads partners to integrate the alliance into their own strategic framework.[24] Trust has also been determined to be a critical component of successful cross-cultural, business-to-business relationships.[25]

More broadly, perceived mutual dependencies can motivate potential partners to come together. Resource dependence theorists have suggested that the development of inter-organizational ties such as strategic alliances result from underlying resource dependencies. Several studies in the 1960s and 1970s showed that an important reason for ties between human service agencies was their perceived strategic interdependence with each other.[26] This research suggested that organizations enter partnerships when they perceive critical strategic interdependence with other organizations in their environment.[27]

More recently, Gulati tested how the social context emerging from prior alliances and considerations of strategic interdependence influence partnership decisions between firms.[28] He found that this social network facilitates new alliances by providing valuable information to firms about the specific capabilities and reliability of potential partners. He also found that connected firms would enter alliances more frequently if the firms were interdependent to begin with and that there would thus be interactions between interdependence and common ties and between interdependence and distance.

This research on the antecedents of alliances among private or nonprofit organizations has compelling implications for understanding corporate–NGO collaboration. Trust, prior experience and perceived interdependence would all appear to influence decisions by companies and NGOs to consider a collaborative relationship.

It is important to note that engagement in a cross-sector alliance presents challenges for both corporate and NGO participants. Corporations and NGOs have fundamentally different structures and values.[29] Relations between corporations and NGOs have often been characterized by hostility and mistrust. Cross-sector alliances face an additional challenge because organizational learning generally requires some level of common experience, a condition that is often weak or missing in alliances between profit-making and nonprofit organizations.[30] This lack of common experience, trust and communication can sometimes result in conflict, even when partnerships appear to have shared values and commitments. Indeed, partnerships with NGOs may sometimes open a path to escalating (and potentially unrealistic) demands for firms to upgrade their commitment to social development, placing greater, not lesser, regulatory pressure on the firm.

Collaboration from the corporate perspective

In the prior chapter, we identified some unique strengths of NGOs that make them daunting adversaries. There are four particularly important NGO strengths that can provide benefits to corporations in the context of a collaborative relationship. They are legitimacy, awareness of social forces, distinct networks and specialized technical expertise. The public bestows the first, and the second is a function of the NGOs' mission. The latter two refer to competences that NGOs have developed by venturing where corporations usually do not go.

Strengths NGOs bring to corporations

Legitimacy
According to a poll conducted by the Edelman public relations firm, both Americans and Europeans said they found NGO spokespeople more credible than either a company's CEO or PR representative. Some fraction of the public, especially in Europe, sees NGOs as dedicated first and foremost to serving an aspect of the general social welfare. While many companies produce direct benefits to society – those in the pharmaceutical and food industries being obvious examples – the public interprets those benefits as byproducts of the companies' profit motive rather than as the direct result of their desire to feed or care for their fellow human beings.

Suspicion of companies' motives can become so entrenched that the soundest solutions are not given a fair hearing. The fate of Shell Oil's Brent Spar storage and tanker offloading system is one such example. After conducting a thorough analysis of what to do with the platform, Shell concluded that towing it into the deep water of the North Atlantic and then sinking it was the best alternative from an environmental standpoint. (It would also be £40 million cheaper than dismantling the platform on land.) Outraged by the plan, Greenpeace organized a boycott of Shell products in the UK and sent protesters to occupy the facility. Ultimately, Shell succumbed to public pressure and hauled the rig ashore for dismantling. Greenpeace subsequently admitted that it had overstated the amount of oil residues in the tank and thus the harmful environmental effects of scuttling.

Awareness of social forces

Companies live and die by the markets they compete in; NGOs, by the ebb and flow of people's concerns about the safety and fairness of conditions worldwide. Although the gulf between the two arenas is large, businesses can learn much from NGOs' atonement to and influence on shifts in common beliefs and mores that in turn shape consumer demand.

For example, in the early 1970s, years before organizations such as PETA were organizing boycotts of fur apparel, and guerrillas from the Animal Liberation Front were infiltrating mink farms to free the animals caged there, groups such as Animal Rights International had highlighted industrial conditions afflicting animals generally. If fur, cosmetics, poultry and fast-food companies had noted the public's first stirrings of humane concern, they could have modified their practices and avoided the ensuing bad publicity and economic harm.

Distinct networks

Most companies' networks primarily consist of organizations that would belong among Michael Porter's five forces model of buyers, suppliers, rival firms, new entrants and substitute producers. NGOs' networks, by contrast, mostly consist of other NGOs, as well as donors, regulators, legislators and public-interest lobbyists. These networks are often quite extensive and dense, since many NGOs are small, lack resources and must form coalitions to be effective. Partnering with NGOs is an excellent way to gain access to the information circulating within their networks.

Specialized technical expertise

NGO members are often thought of as young, unsophisticated malcontents. In reality, the more established NGOs are filled with lawyers, policy analysts and scientists. Half the employees of the largest, most influential environmental NGOs have master's or law degrees, and 10–20 percent have doctorates. Many of them possess knowledge that the companies being targeted lack. The NGOs may know about a new technology that is superior only in its environmental impact and therefore escaped businesses' attention. Or they may have noticed a judicial ruling in an out-of-the-way jurisdiction that may one day set a standard of conduct nationwide. Out of fear that their own research into ways of mitigating harm might establish liability, companies are sometimes willfully ignorant of developments that NGOs are aggressively pursuing.

Benefits to be accrued through collaboration

There are five primary benefits to partnering with NGOs, including to: (1) head off trouble, (2) accelerate innovation, (3) foresee shifts in demand, (4) shape legislation and (5) set industry standards. These factors are discussed in detail as follows:

Head off trouble

Although NGOs are known for engineering confrontations, the more established NGOs increasingly recognize that negotiating directly with companies is more efficient than putting on a negative campaign in hopes that the public will then pressure government officials or the companies themselves to correct the situation they have created. From the companies' standpoint as well, the involvement of motivated experts in place of committed adversaries makes negotiation a more promising alternative.

For example, Doctors Without Borders provides a reliable, efficient and trustworthy partner for pharmaceutical companies in distributing medications in developing countries. Partnering with the NGO also yields reputation benefits. For some corporations, demonstrated commitment to social development may be a precondition for market entry or a de facto requirement for maintaining market presence – a license to operate.

As soon as the first signs of disagreement with a project proposal are in evidence – whether it be a letter to the editor, a petition or a picket line – the company under scrutiny should invite the critics in for a discussion. Even better, companies should learn the concerns of the

NGOs that follow their industry and sound them out while a potentially controversial project is still on the drawing board.

Such is the method currently employed by Shell, which regularly brings together interested groups such as the WWF, Amnesty International and local NGOs at the initial stages of project planning and evaluation. As the ex-chairman of Shell stated, "Brent Spar led us to a new approach in which we try to prevent crises through open dialogue. The discussions aren't always easy, but there is a reasonable amount of mutual trust and understanding between us now."[31] An added benefit, according to the executive, is that the company now has an open channel of communication with the NGOs that attacked it in earlier controversies. If consultations occur regularly instead of during times of crisis, confrontation is less likely.

Consultations should include all interested parties, all gathered around the same table. That way, the party urging an NGO to soften its demands may not be the company itself but a fellow NGO. After all, different NGOs represent different interests. Some groups focus on human rights, some on the protection of endangered species, some on community concerns. When a large-scale project produces diverse results, certain NGOs can end up favoring it and others opposing it. For instance, a factory being planned might bring jobs to the local population but acid rain to the adjoining state. Two NGOs could assess the hazards and benefits differently, even though their networks overlap.

Private negotiation is preferable to public demonstrations, especially when it concerns projects that have not yet been made public. The two have trouble coexisting, since public posturing by either party can erode the trust and candor that are essential for progress to occur in private.

If a company's reputation turns out to be bad enough, most NGOs will refuse to negotiate with it for fear they will lose their bona fides. Some may be willing but will keep quiet about it. One environmental NGO has a partnership with a global fast-food corporation. The NGO provides it with technical guidance on reducing waste. Many environmentalists think its standard practices place it beyond the pale, so the NGO does not talk about the partnership. As a senior executive of the NGO tells it, "We think this partnership is a good thing. It accords with our mission. But not all of our supporters would be thrilled at the association. We don't lie about it, but it just isn't an activity that we advertise."[32] Companies with decent records that acquire a reputation for approachability will generally raise their standing among responsible NGOs. And such companies will obtain valuable exposure to NGOs' concerns and ways of thinking.

Accelerate innovation

In the absence of a dire competitive threat, most companies are content to make incremental improvements to their processes or products. By focusing on the wider effects of companies' practices rather than on their costs or profitability, NGOs are able to demand more of an enterprise than it sometimes demands of itself. The result can be radical solutions that improve some aspect of society or the environment while also increasing competitiveness.

The creation of a market for liquefied petroleum gas (LPG) refrigerators occurred in just this way. In response to the Montreal Protocol's call for eliminating ozone-destroying chlorofluorocarbons by 1996, the chemical industry encouraged appliance makers to replace them with hydrochlorofluorocarbons (HCFCs), greenhouse gases with less ozone-destroying potential. DuPont and ICI, the specialty product and paint developer, invested more than $500 million in research into HCFCs and facilities for manufacturing them.

But in 1991, Greenpeace convinced DKK Scharfenstein, an appliance manufacturer in eastern Germany, to develop a refrigerator based on LPG. The environmentally conscious German consumer market embraced DKK Scharfenstein's refrigerators containing the new technology. By 1994, Bosch and Liebherr, two of Germany's largest appliance makers, had moved almost exclusively to LPG-based refrigerators. Today, refrigerators with LPG technology dominate the markets in many European countries.

Foresee shifts in demand

NGOs often lead social movements. They detect latent but burgeoning concern about an issue, which they then amplify. New norms and values emerge that will, eventually, influence consumers' tastes. Ultimately, they can endanger entire industries. For example, the nuclear energy and genetically modified food industries have become embattled and shrunken at least in part because of NGO-sponsored campaigns highlighting the dangers they pose. Such movements can also direct consumers to substitutes that become the basis of new growth industries.

Take the $10 billion organic foods business, which has been enjoying annual growth rates of 20–30 percent for the past decade. By the time Monsanto and other companies began introducing genetically modified foods to the European market in hopes of launching their own kind of growth industry, a public already traumatized by mad cow disease had become acutely conscious of the safety and purity of the food it ate. Then NGOs such as Friends of the Earth and Greenpeace publicized the dangers of cross-pollination and the threat to butterflies and other insects (see Case illustration on p. 46).

Flush with their success in the US (where, for example, half the soybean crop is genetically modified), the companies producing genetically modified foods failed to take the true measure of Europeans' resistance. Within just a few years, government regulation and public distaste had driven genetically modified foods from Europe's store shelves. By consulting with NGOs, producers of these foods could have avoided investing in a market that was simply not interested and saved themselves billions of dollars.

NGOs are good at sensing shifts in taste and values. They should be, since they are usually born during one of those shifts and depend for their survival on keeping up with them. But NGOs do not simply respond to those shifts. In a positive feedback loop, they help redirect and control them. By staying close to groups that are expert at following and shaping public opinion, companies maintain an advantage, either in their product development or their marketing.

Shape legislation

Through its tax policies, regulation of competition, grants of patent protection and promulgation of labor and environmental standards, to name just some of its powers, government is perhaps the greatest nonmarket-force shaping industry. NGOs have access to like-minded legislators and regulators that even the best-connected corporate lobbyists may not know well. Often, NGOs hear of behind-the-scenes maneuvering or legislative initiatives brewing long before they reach the committee level, and they are sometimes willing to report these to companies they trust. The result is usually better-informed legislation.

Some NGOs are formidable lobbying organizations in their own right. As a WWF executive in Brussels explained to Yaziji, "When I speak with EU lawmakers, I can reasonably claim to be speaking on behalf of 5 million fee-paying members. Politicians listen." Thus, by working with NGOs, companies can have a greater impact on future legislation than they would if they were speaking strictly on behalf of their own economic interests and in opposition to what may be society's wellbeing. An appreciation of the other side's perspective permits the brokering of interests that often precedes the writing of new law. Both companies and NGOs know that they can gain far greater influence by bringing an opponent into their coalition than by adding yet one more industry member or supporter.

Set industry standards
Cooperating with NGOs gives companies a chance not only to avoid various kinds of trouble but also to reshape their industry, sometimes for their own benefit. They can do this by establishing new technology standards, as DKK Scharfenstein happened to do when it developed its new kind of refrigerator. These technology standards then become the basis of new labor or environmental standards, which are enforced either by government mandate or market preference.

Unilever pursued this strategy in its groundbreaking partnership with the WWF. The two organizations joined forces to deal with a serious decline in fisheries around the world. Both knew that voluntary restraint on the part of some fleets would have no effect on the number of fish caught, since the other fleets would increase their catches accordingly – a classic problem of the commons. Yet all of them would suffer economically as the size of their catches shrank or their voyages ranged farther and lasted longer. The two organizations got together in 1996 to develop precise standards for responsible and sustainable fishing practices. Since its founding in 1999, the Marine Stewardship Council (MSC) has accredited more than 100 companies, in twenty countries, which adhere to its standards. Accreditation gives those companies the right to put the MSC logo on their products.

In collaboration with NGOs, industries ranging from coffee production to clothing manufacturing to forestry have established similar certification programs. Aside from protecting the natural resources on which participating businesses depend, the programs have in effect created categories of sought-after products defined by the label they carry. Environmentally minded consumers, for instance, will prefer a can of tuna labeled "dolphin free" over one simply labeled "light tuna."

A reputation for advancing the common good is not the only benefit that accrues to first movers. By setting demanding standards, they present their competitors with a dilemma: either invest large amounts of capital in meeting those standards or face condemnation for refusing to do so. For would-be attackers outside the market in question, standards can serve as barriers to entry.

If a firm dominates its market, it might want to set a technical standard that less well-capitalized competitors would have to struggle to afford, or that applies to an area in which they would prefer not to compete. If a firm does not dominate its market but deploys a technology that is safer or cleaner than its rivals', it may want to work at getting that technology adopted as the new regulatory standard. NGOs should be willing to assist the firm in this.

Being a first mover allows a firm to generate standards that are rational, practicable and uniform. When markets fall into line behind such standards, they reduce the danger that more than one jurisdiction or regulatory body, each with its own idiosyncratic notions, will step in. In the US in particular, where the fifty states as well as the federal government often exercise regulatory oversight, compliance can be difficult and expensive when a single industry standard does not prevail.

A caveat is in order. Credible NGOs will often insist on higher standards of behavior than a firm left to its own devices would choose. In short, an NGO endorsement may not come cheaply.

Risks and challenges

Even when partnerships with NGOs are possible, they carry their own risks. First, if a company interacts with NGOs, it is likely providing them, and by extension its competitors and regulators, with sensitive information. Knowledge of R&D projects, strategic plans and internal audits may help NGOs be better partners, but it might also make them dangerous ones. Just as companies have disclosure policies for joint ventures, they should have strict guidelines for partnerships with NGOs.

Second, partnering with NGOs, and advertising it, can draw stricter scrutiny from the public, the press, regulators and so on than a company formerly received. A lapse that earlier would not have been noteworthy will suddenly call into question a company's sincerity, making further cooperation with NGOs difficult. Worse, cynics are likely to accuse a company of being interested exclusively in image building. CorpWatch, a corporate watchdog, gives out so-called

Greenwash Awards to corporations that "put more money, time, and energy into slick PR campaigns aimed at promoting their eco-friendly images than they do in actually protecting the environment."[33] In short, an overriding interest in good public relations can have the perverse result of actually damaging a company's reputation.

Finally, Berger *et al.* identify several "mis-es" that characterize six predictable problems in corporate–NGO collaborations: misunderstandings, misallocation of costs and benefits, mismatches of power, mismatched partners, misfortunes of time and mistrust.[34]

Best practices

Partnering with an NGO requires nothing less than a change in mentality. In our experience, otherwise highly competent executives find themselves at sea when they venture into the sociopolitical realm, which operates according to its own set of rules. Ask an executive his ultimate responsibility, and he will probably say, "Maximize shareholder return." NGOs – with fundamentally different assumptions about the free market and the role of corporations in society – will see that answer as the problem. And they will act accordingly.

Just as most progressive NGOs take into consideration companies' economic realities when they work to formulate their goals, companies must incorporate an understanding of NGOs' values and concerns into their ordinary cost–benefit calculations.

Hess, Rogovsky and Dunfee argue that in designing corporate social initiatives, companies should seek projects that:

1. Are connected to the firm's core values.
2. Are legitimate responses to moral pressure.
3. Are connected to the core competencies of the firm.
4. Set clear objectives and means of measurement.[35]

Pearce and Doh extend and elaborate on these ideas, offering five principles of collaborative initiatives from the perspective of the corporate partner that they argue are prerequisites for such partnerships to have a discernable impact.[36] These include:

1. *Pursue a durable mission and participate over the long term.* Pearce and Doh argue that companies make the greatest social contribution when they pursue a durable mission and participate

over the long term. They cite education, the environment, health, housing and hunger as examples of social problems that will demand attention for years to come. The Avon Foundation's Breast Cancer Crusade is an example of a long-term commitment to a pervasive problem. Begun in the UK in 1992, it has expanded to fifty countries. Funds are raised through a variety of programs, product sales and special events, including the Avon Walk for Breast Cancer series. To date, the Crusade has awarded more than $300 million to breast cancer research and care organizations worldwide.

2. *Leverage core capabilities: contribute "what we do."* Pearce and Doh suggest that companies maximize the benefits of their corporate contributions when they contribute products and services that are based on expertise developed from their normal operations. They reference IBM's Reinventing Education Program as an example of a partnership that leverages its technological and systems expertise, and its experience providing systems solutions for educational clients, to address a broader educational challenge.

3. *Contribute specialized services to a large-scale undertaking.* Companies have the greatest social impact when they make specialized contributions to large-scale cooperative efforts, according to Pearce and Doh. Firms that contribute to initiatives in which other private, public or nonprofit organizations are also active have an impact that goes beyond their limited contributions. They cite ConAgra Foods Inc.'s partnership with America's Second Harvest, an organization that leads the food recovery effort in the US, as an example of this principle.

4. *Consider government support or minimize interference.* Although some view corporate–NGO partnerships as reactions to the absence of government commitment in a given area, Pearce and Doh argue that government support for corporate participation with NGOs can have an important positive influence. Government tax incentives, liability protection and other forms of direct and indirect support for businesses foster business participation and contribute to the success of cross-sector initiatives (CSIs). Pearce and Doh cite Home Depot Inc.'s partnership with Habitat for Humanity, which is actively supported by the US Department of Housing and Urban Development (HUD) as an illustration of this principle at work.[37]

5. *Assemble and value the total package of benefit.* Finally, Pearce and Doh contend that companies gain the greatest benefits from

their social contributions when they value the total benefit package. Such a valuation should include both the social contributions delivered and the reputation effects that solidify or enhance the company's position among its constituencies. PricewaterhouseCoopers' Project Ulysses is a leadership development program that sends small teams of PwC partners into developing countries to apply their business expertise to complex social and economic challenges. The cross-cultural PwC teams work on a pro bono basis in field assignments for eight weeks with NGOs, community-based organizations and trans-governmental agencies in communities struggling with the effects of poverty, conflict and environmental degradation. This initiative has generated positive value for the firm's effort to attract, retain and develop managerial talent, and to bolster the firm's reputation with clients and regulators, and has contributed to improved morale.

Other researchers also offer lessons for corporations that are targeted by NGOs. Drawing from his analysis of Starbucks' interactions with various NGOs, Argenti offers the following "lessons" for corporate–NGO collaboration from the company's perspective:

Lesson 1: Realize that socially responsible companies are likely targets but also attractive candidates for collaboration.
Lesson 2: Don't wait for a crisis to collaborate.
Lesson 3: Think strategically about relationships with NGOs.
Lesson 4: Recognize that collaboration involves some compromise.
Lesson 5: Appreciate the value of the NGOs' independence.
Lesson 6: Understand that building relationships with NGOs takes time and effort.
Lesson 7: Think more like an NGO by using communication strategically.[38]

Collaboration from the NGO perspective

In their review of the evolution of development NGOs, Brown and Kalegaonkar observe that material resource scarcity is one of the chief challenges facing NGOs and that the collaboration with the business community is one solution to the problem in an era of declining resources for the state.[39] Although many NGOs have challenged business practices that exploit marginalized groups, they have increasingly mobilized resources from businesses to implement programs valued by both NGOs and business. They give the example of commercial bank support for NGO educational innovations in Brazil as one example. They also observe that strategic alliances that advance the core goals of both parties, such as the initiatives of Philippine Business for Social Progress, contribute to political stability for the business community and sustainable development for grassroots groups.

Lindenberg and Dobel echo Brown and Kalegaonkar's interpretation of the response of the NGO sector to the challenges of globalization.[40] In particular, they report that NGOs have emerged to fill voids in the declining role and impact of national government commitment to development support and of outmoded international institutions. Yet, "Ironically, without a state to actually provide services or security, NGOs face the task of how to rebuild communities and provide service often without the effective public power needed to sustain them."[41] They argue that "New technology, declining public resources and unmet needs of refugees and poverty populations have resulted in the growth of NGOs around the world" and that this "creates major dilemmas in how to cooperate with state and corporate sectors in gaining resources."[42] Lindenberg and Dobel note that much of the new corporate wealth is "resolutely antistatist and more inclined to work with the NGO sector. New partnerships between corporations and NGOs are being developed in various communities around the world."[43]

Despite the obvious funding benefits, NGOs may also experience reputation and legitimacy gains. Some NGOs are perceived as fringe, peripheral, inflexible and ineffective so an affiliation with a corporation in good public standing may mitigate some of these perceptions. Perhaps more likely, NGOs may suffer reputation costs and accusations that they have modified or softened their positions in exchange for corporate donations. This "greenwashing" has emerged as a genuine concern for many NGOs seeking to maintain independence and autonomy while engaging corporations for both resources and expertise.

Lindenberg's research has suggested that "NGOs and private sector organizations have had difficulty developing strong and sustainable partnerships."[44] Building on Austin's continuum,[45] Lindenberg asserts that because of distrust between potential partners, few NGO–business relationships have progressed to the integrated stage. However, it is likely that by the end of the next decade, more extensive transactional and integrative partnerships will be in evidence.

NGOs also have reason to be concerned about the net benefits that may accrue to them from relations with corporations. Indeed, according to one study, costs appear to outweigh the benefits. Ashman examined ten cases of collaboration between civil society organizations (NGOs) engaged in development and businesses in Brazil, India and South Africa.[46] Her findings suggest "a sobering view of the benefits that civil society organizations and their constituencies can expect from collaboration."[47] Somewhat paralleling Pearce and Doh's observations on the corporate side,[48] Ashman finds that development impacts are more likely in sectors related to business interests, such as education and employment generation. She also finds that capacity-building objectives are more likely to be realized than are those of citizen empowerment. Finally, NGOs tend to absorb the bulk of the costs of collaboration while businesses often dominate decision-making.

Innovation, dynamism and evolution in corporate–NGO relations

Factors influencing collaboration

Increasingly, NGOs are engaging in both collaborative and combative relationships with corporations. Lindenberg and Dobel summarize the dilemma these closer ties pose for NGOs: "The NGOs face a continuing agenda of how to maintain their mission, integrity and autonomy even as they seek these funds. At the same time they need to protect their own legitimacy in the eyes of funders and recipients and not be used by states or corporations for their own purposes."[49] In response, many NGOs are no longer willing to adopt an either/or approach to their interactions with companies. Rather, they have assumed an increasingly sophisticated and multifaceted relationship with business firms. In moving into this more complex role, they must ask, "When does it make sense to cooperate with the corporate sector and when might it be necessary to provide contravening pressure?"[50]

Similarly, companies are now more strategically evaluating their decisions to engage in collaboration with NGOs. Drawing on resource dependency theory and theories of social networks and social capital,

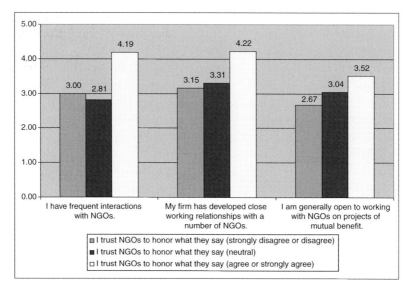

Figure 7.2 Relationship between managers' trust of NGOs and frequency/intensity of collaboration (adapted from J. P. Doh, "Corporate social responsibility through collaboration with NGOs: The role of managerial perceptions and experiences," working paper (2006))

1 = strongly disagree, 2 = disagree, 3 = neither agree nor disagree, 4 = agree and 5 = strongly agree.

Doh reports the results of a survey of *Fortune 500* managers on their perceptions of NGOs and the factors that contribute to decisions to collaborate, as well as the satisfaction with collaboration.[51] He finds that corporate–NGO interactions are common, dynamic and sophisticated, that managers have significant discretion in their approach to NGOs and that managerial perceptions toward NGOs appear to be shaped by their own experiences and that of their companies. The analysis suggests a close linkage between the demographic, experiential and network relationships associated with individual managers and their inclination to engage with NGOs. Age, experience, education and prior affiliation with NGOs are all associated positively with managerial responses regarding the frequency and intensity of their interactions with NGOs and their assessment of the efficacy of those experiences. In addition, perceptions of NGOs as trustworthy and reciprocal partners also positively affect the reported frequency by managers regarding their interactions with NGOs and the positive feelings they have about them. Perhaps more importantly, the perceptions and experiences of managers are correlated with the actions of their firms; the more experience individuals have in interacting with NGOs, the more likely they were to report high levels of interactions by their firms.

Figures 7.2 and 7.3 show the relationship between managers' trust of NGOs and the frequency and intensity of their and their firm's interactions with NGOs, as well as their overall perception of NGOs and reported experiences of working with them. Figure 7.2 shows that the higher trust (defined as trusting NGOs to honor what they say) executives have of NGOs, the more open they are to working with them and the more likely it is that the company for whom they work has developed close working relationships with NGOs. Similarly, those executives who exhibit higher trust of NGOs are also more likely to view NGOs as having a positive impact on society and to see them as generally reliable partners (Figure 7.3).

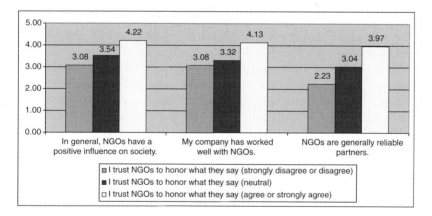

Figure 7.3 Relationship between managers' trust of NGOs and perception of NGOs and satisfaction with collaboration (adapted from J. P. Doh, "Corporate social responsibility through collaboration with NGOs: The role of managerial perceptions and experiences," working paper (2006))

1 = strongly disagree, 2 = disagree, 3 = neither agree nor disagree, 4 = agree and 5 = strongly agree.

Conclusion

Building on our discussions in previous chapters regarding the strategies and operational characteristics of NGOs, in this chapter, we have reviewed the range of interactions among corporations and NGOs. We have highlighted the collaborative connections between corporations and NGOs, despite some conflicting tendencies, and surveyed literature that has examined the dynamic evolution of these relations. Corporate–NGO exchanges are becoming increasingly complex, variegated and fluid; indeed, we have outlined how a given relationship between a firm and NGO may evolve or devolve depending on context, the respective strategies of the stakeholders and other conditions.

In the next chapter, we provide several concrete illustrations of corporate–NGO interactions that reflect these varied connections. We focus on several specific cases that underscore the dynamic and evolutionary nature of corporate–NGO relationships.

Notes

1 J. P. Doh and H. Teegen, "Private investment in emerging markets telecommunications infrastructure: Global trends, national policies, firm strategy," *Competition and Change* 7 (1) (2003), 39–60; D. Hess, N. Rogovsky and T. W. Dunfee, "The next wave of corporate community involvement: Corporate social initiatives," *California Management Review* 44 (2) (2002), 110–125; D. Rondinelli and T. London, "How corporations and environmental groups collaborate: Assessing cross-sector collaborations and alliances," *Academy of Management Executive* 17 (2003), 61–76.

2 B. Kogut and U. Zander, "Knowledge of the firm and the evolutionary theory of the multinational corporation," *Journal of International Business Studies* 24 (4) (1993), 625–645.

3 J. W. Selsky and B. Parker, "Cross-sector partnerships to address social issues: Challenges to theory and practice," *Journal of Management* 31 (6) (2005), 850.

4 Hess, Rogovsky and Dunfee, "The next wave," 110.

5 Selsky and Parker, "Cross-sector partnerships," 849–873.

6 S. A. Waddock, "Building successful social partnerships," *Sloan Management Review* 29 (4) (1988), 17–23; S. Waddock, "A typology of social partnership organizations," *Administration & Society* 22 (4) (1991), 480–516.

7 S. Waddell, "New institutions for the practice of corporate citizenship: Historical, intersectoral, and developmental perspectives," *Business and Society Review* 105 (1) (2000), 107–126.

8 I. E. Berger, P. H. Cunningham and M. E. Drumwright, "Social alliances: Company/nonprofit collaboration," *California Management Review* 47 (1) (2004), 58–90.

9 D. Austrom and L. Lad, "Issues management alliances: New responses, new values, and new logics," *Research in Corporate Social Performance and Policy* 11 (1989), 233–255.

10 D. Ashman, "Civil society collaboration with business: Bringing empowerment back in," *World Development* 29 (7) (2001), 1097–1114.

11 Selsky and Parker, "Cross-sector partnerships," 849–873.

12 J. S. Harrison, M. A. Hitt, R. E. Hoskisson and R. D. Ireland, "Resource complementarity in business combinations: Extending the logic to organizational alliances," *Journal of Management* 27 (6) (2001), 679–690.

13 T. K. Das and B. S. Teng, "Between trust and control: Developing confidence in partner cooperation in alliances," *Academy of Management Review* 23 (3) (1998), 491–512; K. M. Eisenhardt and C. B. Schoonhoven, "Resource-based view of strategic alliance formation: Strategic and social effects in entrepreneurial firms," *Organizational Science* 7 (2) (1996), 136–150.

14 P. Argenti, "Collaborating with activists: How Starbucks works with NGOs," *California Management Review* 47 (1) (2004), 91–116.

15 J. Austin, *The Collaboration Challenge: How Nonprofits and Businesses Succeed through Strategic Alliances* (San Francisco: Jossey-Bass, 2000).

16 Austin, *The Collaboration Challenge*.

17 M. Lindenberg, "Reaching beyond the family: New nongovernmental organization alliances for global poverty alleviation and emergency response," *Nonprofit and Voluntary Sector Quarterly* 30 (2001), 603–615.

18 Selsky and Parker, "Cross-sector partnerships," 849–873.

19 Selsky and Parker, "Cross-sector partnerships," 850–851.

20 P. Mirvis and B. Googins, "Stages of corporate citizenship," *California Management Review* 48 (2) (2006), 104–126.

21 See Rondinelli and London, "How corporations and environmental," 61–76.

22 J. P. Doh and H. Teegen (eds.), *Globalization and NGOs: Transforming Business, Government and Society* (Westport: Praeger, 2003); D. L. Spar and L. T. La Mure, "The power of activism: Assessing the impact of NGOs on global business," *California Management Review* 45 (2003), 78–101; M. Yaziji, "Turning gadflies into allies," *Harvard Business Review* February (2004), 110–115.

23 R. S. Burt, "The network structure of social capital," *Research in Organizational Behavior* 22 (2000), 345–423.

24 J. L. Johnson, J. B. Cullen, T. Sakano and H. Takenouchi, "Setting the stage for trust and strategic integration in Japanese-U.S. cooperative alliances," *Journal of International Business Studies* 27 (5) (1996), 981–1005.

25 T. Heffernan, "Trust formation in cross-cultural business-to-business relationships," *Qualitative Market Research* 7 (2) (2004), 114.

26 For a review, see C. Oliver, "Determinants of interorganizational relationships: Integration and future directions," *Academy of Management Review* 15 (1990), 241–265.

27 J. R. Schermerhorn Jr., "Determinants of interorganizational cooperation," *Academy of Management Journal* 18 (1975), 846–856; D. A. Whetten, "Toward a contingency model for designing interorganizational service delivery systems," *Organization and Administrative Sciences* 4 (1977), 77–96.

28 R. Gulati, "Social structure and alliance formation patterns: A longitudinal analysis," *Administrative Science Quarterly* 40 (4) (1995), 619–652.

29 Rondinelli and London, "How corporations and environmental," 61–76.

30 Rondinelli and London, "How corporations and environmental," 61–76.

31 Sir Mark Moody-Stuart, personal communication, October (2001).

32 Greenpeace, executive interview (2001).

33 "Corpwatch: Greenwash Awards," available at www.corpwatch.org/ article.php?list=type&type=102. Accessed January 26, 2008.

34 Berger, Cunningham and Drumwright, "Social alliances," 58–90.

35 Hess, Rogovsky and Dunfee, "The next wave," 110–125.

36 J. A. Pearce III and J. P. Doh, "The high impact of collaborative social initiatives," *Sloan Management Review* 46 (2) (2005), 30–39.

37 Pearce III and Doh, "The high impact," 30–39.

38 Argenti, "Collaborating with activists," 110–113.

39 L. D. Brown and A. Kalegaonkar, "Support organizations and the evolution of the NGO sector," *Nonprofit and Voluntary Sector Quarterly* 31 (2002), 231–258.

40 M. Lindenberg and P. J. Dobel, "The challenges of globalization for northern international relief and development NGOs," *Nonprofit and Voluntary Sector Quarterly* 28 (1999), 8.

41 Lindenberg and Dobel, "The challenges of globalization," 11.

42 Lindenberg and Dobel, "The challenges of globalization," 11.

43 Lindenberg and Dobel, "The challenges of globalization," 12.

44 Lindenberg, "Reaching beyond the family," 605.

45 Austin, *The Collaboration Challenge*.

46 Ashman, "Civil society collaboration," 1097–1114.
47 Ashman, "Civil society collaboration," 1097.
48 Pearce III and Doh, "The high impact," 30–39.
49 Lindenberg and Dobel, "The challenges of globalization," 12.
50 Lindenberg and Dobel, "The challenges of globalization," 12.
51 J. P. Doh, "Corporate social responsibility through collaboration with NGOs: The role of managerial perceptions and experiences," Working paper (2006).

8 | Globalization, multinationals and NGOs: the next wave

The process of globalization is not a new phenomenon, but stretches back centuries. Globalization, on the other hand, encompasses a vision of integrating social, political, economic, cultural and technological aspects to create a unified world market. According to Friedman, as globalization becomes a household word, the world will continue to "flatten" until the globe is virtually an integrated web.[1] However, as the world becomes more integrated, it poses different challenges for established and emergent institutions. Corporations may find it easier to reach the global marketplace, but the myriad of cultures, social values and political structures will leave them vulnerable to NGOs that may not agree with their behavior and conduct.

Globalization and its many reverberations pose new challenges for multinational corporations (MNCs) and NGOs. Debates over the negative spillovers of globalization have not just permeated, but at times dominated, the popular business press. Dozens of books have been published in recent years addressing globalization and its varied impacts, and many of these volumes have become bestsellers.[2] Photographs of police clashing with protesters at meetings of the WTO, the World Economic Forum, the joint meetings of the World Bank and IMF, and many other global assemblies, have been featured on the covers of major dailies and weeklies throughout the world. NGOs have provided the vehicle for organized advocacy in support of a variety of interests impacted by globalization trends. When rock star Bono accompanied Treasury Secretary Paul O'Neil on a tour of Africa to raise awareness of AIDS, debt and trade issues – a trip sponsored in part by Bono's NGO, DATA (Debt, AIDS, Trade for Africa) – international NGO activity was propelled to the front pages of the mainstream press. These images and others reflect concerns of a select group of protesters – and more broadly, of citizens and collectives of stakeholder groups – that the present global economic order, as constructed by international organizations, select national

146

governments and MNCs, does not necessarily serve the interests of broader societies.

In this chapter, we discuss how globalization is affecting corporate–NGO interactions. We begin by briefly reviewing some of the milestones in NGO activism in the modern era, including the South Africa divestment campaign and the boycott of Nestlé infant formula. We continue with a discussion of the emerging role of NGOs in international trade agreements, such as in the dispute over trade in tuna and its impacts on marine mammal protection, and the growing importance of international standards and codes of conduct as a mechanism to advance NGO interests in labor, human rights, the environment and other areas. We then touch upon the increasing influence international and local NGOs may have over MNC entry into new and emerging economies.

Early global NGO activity

The rising influence of NGOs is one of the most significant developments in international affairs over the past twenty years. The modern era of NGO activism can be traced to the 1960s and 1970s when a number of civil rights, environmental and women's groups emerged to advocate for changes in public policy and corporate practices in a range of areas. In addition to the publication of Rachel Carson's *Silent Spring* in 1962, two other important milestones in NGO activism are worth noting.

In the late 1970s, a number of NGOs initiated a boycott of Nestlé over its marketing and distribution of an infant formula.[3] In particular, Nestlé SA was accused by a number of activist investors, such as the Interfaith Center for Corporate Responsibility (ICCR) and NGOs such as the Infant Formula Action Coalition (INFACT), of adopting deceptive hard-sell promotional practices to scare mothers in the developing world into using formula over breast milk.[4] The second development occurred in 1984, when a range of NGOs, including church and community groups, human rights organizations and other anti-apartheid activists, built strong networks and pressed US cities and states to divest their public pension funds of companies doing business in South Africa. By the end of 1989, twenty-six states, twenty-two counties and over ninety cities had taken some form of binding economic action that, when combined with broader public pressure, helped generate the thrust for passage of the 1986 Comprehensive Anti-Apartheid Act over the veto of President Reagan. The Act banned new US investment in South Africa, export sales to the police and military and new bank loans, except to support trade. The combination of domestic unrest, international governmental pressures and capital flight posed a direct, sustained and ultimately successful challenge to the white minority rule, resulting in the collapse of apartheid.[5]

NGOs and international economic policy

NGOs have increasingly pushed to have greater access to the trade policy process, a system that has historically been limited to governments acting as agents of business, and, to a lesser degree, representatives of labor interests. NGOs have expressed a great deal of interest in the trade policy dispute settlement mechanism under the General Agreement on Tariffs and Trade (GATT) and its successor agreement, the WTO. An important milestone in NGOs' influence over the international trade regime was the so-called tuna-dolphin case, mentioned earlier. This case was somewhat of a landmark in launching NGO activism in the trade–environmental arena, and also became a cause célèbre in the North American Free Trade Agreement (NAFTA) negotiations.

Under the Marine Mammal Protection Act (MMPA), the US banned the importation of tuna from certain countries, because it was caught in a manner that also caused harm to dolphins. The US faced a GATT challenge from Mexico and Venezuela, two of the countries from which tuna had been banned over these restrictions.[6] The panel ruled against the US in both cases, in 1991 and 1992, and the reaction from environmental NGOs constituted a rallying cry to efforts by activists to gain access to multilateral trade dispute settlement processes, and to incorporate environmental commitments in government-negotiated trade agreements. While the panel decision was never adopted by the GATT members (before the reform of the Dispute Resolution system in the Uruguay Round of multilateral negotiations, adoption of the findings of a panel could be blocked by a single member, including the country found to be in violation), eventually, the matter was resolved through bilateral negotiations that led to the creation of an international dolphin conservation program.

Subsequently, the Uruguay Round agreements explicitly made provisions for cooperation with NGOs. In the Uruguay Round Agreement Establishing the World Trade Organization, Article V(2) on Relations with Other Organizations states that, "The General Council may make appropriate arrangements for consultation and cooperation with nongovernmental organizations concerned with matters related to those of the WTO."[7]

International strategies of NGOs: Countervailing forces and supportive partners

NGOs are becoming more international and developing global operations and strategies that rival their corporate counterparts. In these international efforts, NGOs often gear their advocacy efforts to challenge established actors including governments and firms whose actions may run counter to particular social interests. For example, Keck and Sikkink describe four international political tactics employed by NGOs: information politics, symbolic politics, leverage politics and accountability politics. In each of these tactics, the NGO transforms information into power, typically using media to communicate with the public at large. In information politics, the NGO might pose as an unbiased source of scientific information. In symbolic politics, the NGO transforms an individual event into a symbol for the NGO ideal. Leverage politics uses government to act, pressuring the MNC to adopt a specific policy. Accountability politics holds the MNCs accountable for promises made, making public any lapses in performance. Thus, NGOs may act as agents that confine and restrict MNCs' strategies in developing countries. When NGOs target an industry, corporation or other organization through activism such as boycotts, protests, public campaign and other advocacy efforts, this increases the costs associated with a given MNC strategy.[8]

An effective advocacy effort concerned a consortium of environmental NGOs opposed to the $75 billion Three Gorges Dam project in China due to concerns related to the destruction of hundreds of miles of river and the forcible resettlement of 1.3 million people. As a result, the World Bank, Asian Development Bank and other development and aid organizations decided to withhold funding for the project. This severely compromised the financial feasibility of the project and significantly reduced the opportunities for MNCs to win a piece of the many contracts expected from the project. In addition, MNCs involved in the project suffered reputation effects, and enhanced visibility as they are now the targets of ongoing actions by NGOs.

In January 2004, Citigroup announced it would no longer finance certain projects in emerging markets identified by the Rainforest Action Network (RAN) as damaging to the environment. Specifically, Citigroup will avoid projects involving commercial logging and those that disrupt indigenous populations and will monitor and report the greenhouse gas emissions of the projects it does finance. This announcement came after several years of aggressive pressure and lobbying by RAN, including full-page advertising in daily newspapers showing barren landscapes and blackened trees, lobbying by film and television personalities urging consumers to cut up their credit cards, blockades of Citigroup branches and campaigns involving schoolchildren who sent cards to Citigroup's Chairman, Sanford Weil, asking him to stop contributing to the extinction of endangered species. Citigroup's decision to negotiate the agreement with the RAN regarding future projects it would finance was partly a result of repercussions associated with the China project.[9]

Citizens have come to expect NGOs to serve in a monitoring and oversight role with respect to MNC behavior and activities, including monitoring corporate social and environmental responsibility. NGOs like Oxfam and RAN now investigate and report on MNC pledges and actions in the areas of governance, labor practices, human rights, environmental impact and many others.

NGOs may also serve as supportive partners in MNCs' international expansion. They can provide shelter, convey positive reputation and open avenues to circumvent inefficient, corrupt or bureaucratic governments. Furthermore, they can provide mechanisms to support and facilitate MNC social development efforts and in so doing, strengthen MNC reputation and legitimacy, provide information to ease subsequent market entry, act as brokers in negotiating and coordinating with other parties and lower operating costs.

NGOs pool their resources and capabilities to form broader collectives not only with other NGOs but also with private corporations whose activities are consistent with the pursuit of social welfare. The Global Development Alliance Secretariat, an important pillar in the programmatic offerings of the US Agency for International Development, promotes exactly this type of NGO–MNC engagement for social good. NGOs and MNCs have unique resource sets that can be combined in ways that produce great gains to social welfare alongside promoting the economic value creation purposes of firms. Operationally, NGOs can serve as valuable intermediaries for MNCs working within developing nation economies – as distribution channel partners, aggregators of demand and market information providers.

Some MNCs have therefore decided to work closely with NGOs, and have identified projects that include collaboration with NGOs as an avenue to advance both social and economic goals. Such projects may allow the MNC to experiment, educate, test and grow markets without major investments in infrastructure or other fixed assets. For example, Hewlett Packard Corporation has initiated a series of "i-communities" in economically deprived areas such as the town of Kuppam in the state of Andhra Pradesh, India. These communities use public–private–NGO partnerships to enhance economic development through technology. NGOs promote the projects and enlist community support. HP is able to use the projects to build markets, test products and expand global marketing knowledge. The experience provides HP with valuable knowledge of how to identify and negotiate with rural customers, allowing the firm to reduce search, monitoring and enforcement costs of doing business in rural markets of India and related settings in the future. In addition, HP has received positive reputation effects in development circles.

NGOs may initially target MNCs to urge a change in policy, and subsequently work with those same MNCs to implement, certify or oversee the results of those efforts. For example, multinational processors of commodities such as coffee, cocoa and bananas have been criticized by NGOs for exploitive labor and environmental practices in emerging economies. In response, Chiquita is working with the Rainforest Alliance to certify all of its plantations under RAN's "Better Bananas Project," and Proctor and Gamble and other coffee producers have partnered with Transfair to source "fair trade coffee" that assures responsible labor and environmental standards on coffee plantations, as well as guarantees a minimum price to producers.

NGOs and international agreements and codes

In addition to individual corporate–NGO interactions, NGOs have also been very active in collective efforts to develop, implement and enforce industry-wide standards, codes of conduct and agreements. Such codes have recently been found to have positive, material impacts on developing countries, and even contribute to the avoidance of conflicts which sap developing countries of their stability and potential. According to Doh and Guay, NGO involvement in these agreements can be classified by their principal sponsoring organizations:[10]

1. International agreements signed by governments. Examples include the WTO and NAFTA, each of which has provisions dealing with environmental and labor standards.
2. International codes sponsored by International Governmental Organizations (IGOs). Examples include the UN Global Compact, International Labour Organization (ILO) Declaration of Principles concerning Multinational Enterprises and Social Policy and the Organisation for Economic Cooperation and Development (OECD) Guidelines for MNEs.
3. International codes sponsored by industrial and corporate groups. Examples include the World Business Council for Sustainable Development (WBCSD), Global Environmental Management Institute (GEMI) and ISO 14000 environmental management standards.
4. International codes sponsored by not-for-profit NGOs. Examples include the Social Accountability International SA8000 standard, Rugmark, a standard that certifies rugs and carpets as meeting basic standards for labor and human rights and the Forest Stewardship Council (FSC) standard that certifies lumber as consistent with sustainable practices.

Table 8.1 presents a summary of these international agreements and codes of conduct governing corporate labor and environmental policies and the role of NGOs in theory formulation and compliance. NGOs are involved in all of these, however, it is the last category in which NGOs have the most influence and impact.

International standards and codes of conduct initiated by NGOs or that involve some NGO influence are proliferating. An international conference arranged by the International Center for Corporate Accountability was held in 2004 regarding such voluntary codes of conduct, with a special issue of *Business Ethics Quarterly* featuring several of the papers presented at that conference.[11]

Some have argued that ethical codes of conduct are necessary to counter the perceived abuses by MNCs as they expand abroad,

Table 8.1. *International agreements and codes of conduct governing corporate labor and environmental policies: examples and NGO role in formulation/compliance (adapted from Dob and Guay, "Globalization and corporate social responsibility")*

	International agreements signed by governments	International codes sponsored by IGOs	International codes sponsored by industrial and corporate associations	International codes sponsored by not-for-profit NGOs
Examples	North American Free Trade Agreement, World Trade Organization (WTO), Free Trade Agreement of the Americas	UN Global Compact, ILO Declaration of Principles concerning Multinational Enterprises and Social Policy, OECD Guidelines for MNEs	World Business Council for Sustainable Development (WBCSD), Global Environmental Management Institute (GEMI), ISO 14000	Social Accountability International SA8000, Rugmark, Forest Stewardship Council (FSC)
Representative list of NGOs involved	Environmental (Sierra Club, WWF); labor (AFL-CIO, UAW); corporate (US Chamber of	Labor (Trade Union Advisory Committee to the OECD, International Confederation of Free Trade Unions); environmental (WWF, World Resources Institute,	National chambers of commerce, national technical standards groups (American National Standards Institute), national industry associations,	Labor (The International Textile, Garment and Leather Workers' Federation, Union Network Intl.); development (Save the Children); human rights (Amnesty International);

Table 8.1. (*cont.*)

	International agreements signed by governments (Commerce, National Association of Manufacturers)	International codes sponsored by IGOs (IUCN – the World Conservation Union); human rights (Amnesty, Human Rights Watch)	International codes sponsored by industrial and corporate associations (International Standards Organization)	International codes sponsored by not-for-profit NGOs (environmental (National Resources Defense Council, National Wildlife Federation, WWF))
NGO role in agreement formulation	Low	Low	High	High
NGO role in agreement compliance	Moderate	Low/Moderate	Moderate	High

Many NGOs participate in the above codes on an ad hoc or informal basis.

154

balancing internal corporate capabilities with external societal needs.[12] Others argue that purely voluntary codes of conduct are ineffective.[13] One solution is to encourage mandatory adoption of codes across an industry and to consider codes as the first step in a system of global laws or regulations such that MNCs would ultimately be legally required to uphold, forcing them to be more transparent in order for a system of checks and balances to be put in place.[14]

Codes of conduct may be viewed as a system of self-regulation that could result in a more harmonious global economy.[15] In turn, MNCs would have access to resources that would provide a better balance between their economic performance and societal needs. From a global perspective, the integration of these interests could sustain and potentially improve socially and globally responsible practices and compensate for the ineffective components of purely voluntary corporate codes.[16] Regardless of the methods used to encourage the attractiveness of or the adoption of the voluntary codes, it is in the interest of global communities to further explore a more universal agreement rather than specific, discrete codes affecting a subset of companies within a particular area (environment, labor, human rights).[17]

NGOs and developing countries

As companies expand internationally, they face challenging institutional environments in which political, legal and social institutions are underdeveloped and make entry and operations difficult. These challenges are exacerbated by the MNCs' relative inexperience in the local market, resulting in "liabilities" faced by foreign firms that are not encountered by local, indigenous companies.[18]

Khanna and Palepu discuss these "institutional voids" as a severe liability of doing business in developing countries and one that suggests alternative organizational forms in order to attain effective strategy. Institutional voids arise in locations where specialized intermediaries on which a firm customarily relies – legal, financial, human resources – are absent. Such absences may result from poorly functioning institutional infrastructure and governance systems. One response of firms to these institutional deficits is to internalize functions through the development of business groups or conglomerates that provide internal capital and labor markets and protect property rights by not exposing them to partners. Another alternative is for the MNE to support development of emergent institutions in the nongovernmental sector to fill the gaps generated by these institutional deficits.[19] Alternatively, MNCs can adapt and become "isomorphic" with the local institutional environment.[20]

Another strategy involves engaging with alternative local institutions and contributing to their development so that they might provide the conditions for profitable business. Supporting institutions and therefore investments in developing or bolstering such institutions may yield significant medium- and long-term benefits for the MNE.

In considering relationships between MNEs and local NGOs in developing countries, there are a range of potentially complementary benefits. The MNE brings size, scale, experience and resources and the NGO enables the MNE to access stakeholders that would be difficult to reach without the partnership. Specifically, locally based NGOs may help the MNC learn more about the genuine needs of the host country, to contribute to social development efforts and to gain legitimacy in the host country market. The firm-specific advantages of MNEs may in turn help NGOs and other stakeholder organizations to provide improved products and services to their constituent groups and to provide access to international markets. Together these two organizational forms may be in a position to fill institutional voids because, in many cases, governments in developing countries may simply lack the capacity and resources to create the type of institutions that are able to promote development.

Developing country populations and firms benefit from the international capabilities of MNEs when MNEs partner with local NGOs and other organizations to facilitate direct access to consumers in developed country markets. MNE–NGO collaborations provide producers with opportunities to compress the supply chain and circumvent price mark-ups by intermediaries. They can also facilitate the establishment of premium brand recognition for products produced or harvested and otherwise promote greater awareness and support for developing country working conditions and income needs. Collaboration among MNEs and NGOs can also create emergent institutions at the micro-level to the benefit of both the MNE and the local system. For example, in developing countries, capital market imperfections, lack of knowledge of credit assessment and risk, macroeconomic risk and bureaucratic inefficiencies severely constrain access to credit in poor and rural areas. MNE experience and establishment of parallel – but highly functional – financial infrastructure can improve provision of these services.

In the example above, US-based NGO RAN identified a list of emerging countries that would be most affected by Citigroup's expansion. It lobbied the company, indicating that its operations would contribute to deforestation and species extinction. After years of pressure from this effective NGO, Citibank decided to curb support of commercial logging, report greenhouse gas emissions and reduce dislocation of indigenous populations.[21] This is just one example of how an MNC may yield to the home-country NGO.

NGOs in developing countries are gaining power and influence, which may be in part due to the inadequate societal provisions through governmental power – the institutional voids described above. When NGOs displace host governments, they can have a more direct say over the rights of MNEs to enter and operate in host countries.[22] In these situations, NGOs have substantial bargaining power, triggering a bargaining negotiation among MNCs, NGOs and host governments.[23]

In some instances, the MNC, anticipating potential backlash upon market entry, may reach out to a well-known international NGO and initiate a relationship that may shelter it from local NGO criticism. Many international NGOs have developed strong connections with smaller, local NGOs or larger, national NGOs in order to integrate their global and local priorities.[24] Under this scenario, the MNC is interacting with the larger, more powerful international NGO, but is also receiving input, indirectly, from the local NGOs in order to calibrate its entry strategy so that it is responsive to local concerns. In this way, "Since it is vital for the MNC to achieve and maintain legitimacy in all its environments, the MNC will experience the pressure to adopt local practices and become isomorphic with the local institutional context."[25]

As with other NGO relationships that we have discussed throughout the book, MNCs can engage in either collaborative or combative relationships among international, national and local NGOs upon market entry. The Citigroup example above shows how an NGO can be a potential barrier, increasing entry costs and forcing changes in international strategy. In the case of Doctors Without Borders, however, there was a collaborative arrangement that resulted in reduced costs for delivering AIDS drugs to South African populations when the government did not lend sufficient support. As also noted above, interactions can combine advocacy and collaboration, as was the case in the Chiquita examples, where the company was under scrutiny by NGOs for unfair labor practices in the banana industry but subsequently worked with the Rainforest Alliance on the "Better Bananas Project." Similarly, Proctor and Gamble's collaboration with Transfair in purchasing "fair trade" products, which promise a minimum price to producers and also ensures environmental and labor standards, was also motivated by pressure and criticism from NGOs. These collaborations can increase company legitimacy, reduce costs incurred by long negotiations and searching for suppliers or laborers, and minimize future attacks by local NGOs on the international landscape.

Starbucks has become a well-known MNE with international operations in at least thirty countries outside of the US. Before its vast expansion, a representative from the NGO CARE approached the company in 1991 to inform them of programs and initiatives. Starbucks was already socially aware, and collaborating with such a proactive group seemed to be in the company's best interest. At first, the relationship was transactional in the sense that Starbucks passed on $2 from each sale of coffee samplers to CARE. Over time, the organizations began to integrate, and Starbucks began to consult CARE on codes of conduct and standards in overseas operations. This included Starbucks's choice in engaging in "fair trade" coffee sales, where farmers are adequately compensated for their efforts, instead of investing in operations where there may exist questionable labor practices.[26] These pre-emptive actions by Starbucks enabled it to work with CARE for almost a decade before becoming a fully developed MNE, curbing potential combative relationships with other NGOs.

Conclusion

Globalization poses challenges for corporations (MNCs) and NGOs and raises particular issues around their interactions, especially within developing countries. In this chapter, we have described the evolution of the role of NGOs and corporate–NGO interactions in global environments and highlighted some of the arenas and contexts in which these interactions have been especially intense, such as in international economic policy debates in the WTO and in the development and implementation of corporate codes of conduct. We also explored the specific context of developing countries as a particularly interesting and revealing setting to understand some of the dynamics of corporate–NGO relations which we introduced earlier in the book.

Economic integration among countries will continue to be accompanied by the global expansion of business and, increasingly, of the NGO sector. It seems inevitable that the frequency and intensity of corporate–NGO interactions will be part of this mix.

Notes

1 T. Friedman, *The World is Flat: A Brief History of the Twenty-first Century* (New York: Farrar, Straus and Giroux, 2005).

2 These include Thomas Friedman's *The Lexus and the Olive Tree* (New York: Farrar, Straus and Giroux, 1999); Joseph Stiglitz's, *Globalization and its Discontents* (London: Norton, 2002); Peter Singer's *One World: The Ethics of Globalization* (New Haven: Yale University Press, 2002); George Soros's, *George Soros on Globalization* (New York: Public Affairs, 2002); A. Barber and B. Schulz's *Jihad vs. McWorld: How Globalism and Tribalism are Reshaping the World* (New York: Ballantine, 1996); and many others.

3 See L. H. Newton, "Truth is the daughter of time: The real story of the Nestle case," *Business and Society Review* 104 (1999), 367–395; P. Sethi, *Multinational Corporations and the Impact of Public Advocacy on Corporate Strategy: Nestle and the Infant Formula Controversy* (New York: Kluwer, 1994).

4 Newton, "Truth is the daughter of time," 367–395.

5 R. Wright, "Sanctions, disinvestment, and U.S. corporations in South Africa," in R. Edgar (ed.), *Sanctioning Apartheid* (Trenton: Africa World Press, 1990).

6 See F. Reinhardt and R. Vietor, "Starkist," in F. Reinhardt and R. Vietor (eds.), *Business Management and the Natural Environment* (Cincinnati: South-Western College, 1996), pp. 3, 102, 122.

7 See World Trade Organization (WTO), *Uruguay Round Agreement Establishing the World Trade Organization*, volume 2 (Geneva: World Trade Organization, 1995).

8 M. E. Keck and K. Sikkink. *Activists Without Borders* (Ithaca: Cornell University Press, 1998).

9 "Environmentalists get Citigroup pledge," *New York Times* January 22 (2004), C3.

10 J. P. Doh and T. R. Guay, "Globalization and corporate social responsibility: How nongovernmental organizations influence labor and environmental codes of conduct," *Management International Review* 44 (3) (2004), 7–30.

11 S. Prakash Sethi, "Voluntary codes of conduct for multinational corporations," *Business Ethics Quarterly* 16 (2) (2006), 117.

12 L. M. Sama, "Interactive effects of external environmental conditions and internal firm characteristics on MNE's choice of strategy in the development of a code of conduct," *Business Ethics Quarterly* 16 (2) (2006), 137–165.

13 T. Campbell, "A human rights approach to developing voluntary codes of conduct for multinational corporations," *Business Ethics Quarterly* 16 (2) (2006), 255–269.

14 Campbell, "A human rights approach," 255–269.

15 B. Arya and J. E. Salk, "Cross-sector alliance learning and effectiveness of voluntary codes of corporate social responsibility," *Business Ethics Quarterly* 16 (2) (2006), 211–234.

16 Arya and Salk, "Cross-sector alliance," 211–234.

17 N. Hsieh, "Voluntary codes of conduct for multinational corporations: Coordinating duties of rescue and justice," *Business Ethics Quarterly* 16 (2) (2006), 119–135.

18 S. Zaheer, "Overcoming the liability of foreignness," *Academy of Management Journal* 38 (1995), 341–363.

19 T. Khanna, K. Palepu and J. Sinha, "Strategies to fit emerging markets," *Harvard Business Review* 83 (6) (2005), 63–74.

20 T. Kostova, "Transnational transfer of strategic organizational practices: A contextual perspective," *Academy of Management Review* 24 (1999), 308–324; T. Kostova and K. Roth, "Adoption of an organizational practice by the subsidiaries of the MNC: Institutional and relational effects," *Academy of Management Journal* 45 (2002), 215–233.

21 "Environmentalists get Citigroup pledge," *New York Times* January 22 (2004), C3.

22 J. P. Doh and H. Teegen (eds.), *Globalization and NGOs: Transforming Business, Government, and Society* (Westport: Praeger, 2003).

23 D. J. Encarnation and S. Vachani, "Foreign ownership: When hosts change the rules," *Harvard Business Review* September/October (1985), 152–159; W. J. Henisz and O. E. Williamson, "Comparative economic organization – Within and between countries," *Business and Politics* 1 (1999), 261–277; C. W. L. Hill, P. Hwang and W. C. Kim, "An eclectic theory of choice of international entry mode," *Strategic Management Journal* 11 (2) (1990), 117–128.

24 H. Teegen, "International NGOs as global institutions: Using social capital to impact multinational enterprises and governments," *Journal of International Management* 9 (3) (2003), 271–285.
25 T. Kostova and K. Roth, "Adoption of an organizational practice," 215.
26 M. Lindenberg, "Declining state capacity, voluntarism, and the globalization of the not-for-profit sector," *Nonprofit and Voluntary Sector Quarterly* 28 (1999), 147–167.

Case illustration: conflict diamonds

International advocacy NGOs, such as Global Witness and Amnesty International, are at the forefront of stemming the flow of conflict diamonds. Relationships between corporations and NGOs in this capacity gradually developed from adversarial to collaborative. Global Witness initially waged a negative relationship with Tiffany & Co. by protesting at its businesses and demanding change in the late 1990s. By 2004, however, Global Witness was praising Tiffany & Co. and working alongside businesses with the Kimberley Process Certification Scheme (KPCS). Global Witness has a vast sphere of collaborative influence, evident by the establishment of the KPCS and by continued involvement in and evolution of the project between industry, governmental and NGO representatives. Continued criticism of collaborative efforts reveals that corporate–NGO relationships sometimes suffer from the lack of a shared vision.

In May 2000, under pressure from a mounting movement against "blood diamonds" or "conflict diamonds," the diamond industry convened with government representatives and civil society organizations in Kimberley, South Africa. This movement began in 1998 after Global Witness, an advocacy NGO, led the charge with a large-scale advocacy campaign that included protests outside Tiffany & Co. stores and other retailers. Proceeds from the sales of conflict diamonds are used to fund militias, purchase guns for child soldiers, support resistance of the UN, fund civil wars and cause other human rights violations. "The trade in conflict diamonds has fuelled protracted and bloody wars in Angola, the Democratic Republic of Congo, Liberia and Sierra Leone, destroying nations and costing an estimated 3.7 million lives," said Kate Allen, the director of Amnesty International UK.[1]

After Global Witness launched its campaign, Tiffany & Co. CEO Michael Kowalski shifted into damage control and quickly amended company policies in the face of the criticism. Kowalski says, "It wasn't

162

hard for us to imagine the NGO community focusing on us."[2] As protesters started to line up outside Tiffany stores in 2000, Kowalski had already called his suppliers to ensure that their diamonds were legitimate. Kowalski met with other industry and governmental representatives in Kimberley to negotiate a solution to the problem.

The assembly in Kimberley spawned a series of negotiations between governments, NGOs and diamond industry representatives that led to the Kimberley Process Certification Scheme, an international certification scheme aimed to prevent the trade of conflict diamonds. Eventually launched in January 2003, the sixty countries participating in the KPCS agreed to certify that shipments of diamonds from their countries were free from conflict diamonds. Many members across sectors of the diamond industry agreed to implement a code of conduct to prevent trade of conflict diamonds, to implement a warrant system stating that invoices would declare that diamonds were conflict free and to inform employees of these policies. The collaboration appeared to be a great milestone in corporate–NGO relationships.

However, in the eyes of some NGOs, the agreement was not really implemented, nor did it go far enough. In a co-written 2004 report, Amnesty International and Global Witness criticize industry efforts against conflict diamonds, "Major players in the diamond jewelry retail sector continue to fall short on implementing basic measures of the self regulation." In the report, forty-eight of the eighty-five companies surveyed about their policies on conflict diamonds did not even respond, and the majority of responding companies did not provide adequate details about their policies.[3] Out of 579 US and UK stores, fewer than half had a policy on conflict diamonds and very few provided the warranty certificate confirming that the diamonds were legitimate.[4] Amnesty International and Global Witness ultimately called for government intervention and independent monitoring.

Tiffany & Co., a former main target of Global Witness, stood out positively by providing a detailed response to the Amnesty International and Global Witness survey that described how the company strengthened auditing and sourcing policies to ensure that its diamonds were legitimate. The company recently entered into a contract to buy $30 million worth of diamonds from Aber Diamond Corporation in Canada, providing a source of non-conflict diamonds.[5] One industry insider revealed that Tiffany & Co. would like to source all of its diamonds from Canada.[6] Although primarily a target of protest, Tiffany & Co. now works productively with other NGOs as part of the KPCS.

Tiffany & Co. also faces controversy over its gold-mining processes. Much like he did when conflict diamonds began to be controversial, Kowalski, the CEO, tried to pre-empt more controversy by taking quick action, which has been lauded by Oxfam's "No Dirty Gold campaign."[7] Tiffany & Co. supports environmentally responsible mines, and it even took out a full-page advertisement in the *Washington Post* criticizing plans for two mine projects in the US. Clearly, Tiffany & Co. wants to resolve issues and avoid clashing with NGOs.

Another major company, De Beers, is learning to work with NGOs. It is the largest diamond company in the world, and speaks out against child labor, conflict diamonds and unethical business practices in its best practice principles.[8] Known for its opaque practices, De Beers wields huge power in many of the African countries in which it operates.[9] The company's powerful position has not stopped it from joining forces with Global Witness, Partnership Africa Canada and other NGO and industry organizations to form the Diamond Development Initiative (DDI), announced in August 2005.[10] DDI's mission statement is, "To gather all interested parties into a process that will address, in a comprehensive way, the political, social and economic challenges facing the artisanal diamond mining sector in order to optimize the beneficial development impact of artisanal diamond mining to miners, their communities and their governments."[11] While still nascent, this collaboration seeks to limit conflict diamonds and reach some of the miners still not helped by the Kimberley Process. This relationship is another example of a productive corporate–NGO relationship.

Global Witness and other nongovernmental groups were successful in establishing the Kimberly Process, but voiced criticisms, such as the 2004 study, that the Kimberly Process was not accomplishing enough. This conflict of interests demonstrates that the goals of businesses and NGOs do not always coincide. In November 2005, at the Moscow plenary meeting of the Kimberley Process, the diamond industry and diamond-producing countries did make a strong commitment to slow the smuggling of conflict diamonds from West Africa, to Global Witness's satisfaction. All diamond production from West Africa will now be monitored and exports will be profiled. Global Witness, an outspoken proponent of more action, lauded the move, "This sort of action is long overdue and we hope the promises will be met," said Alex Yearsley of Global Witness.[12]

These changes in the supply chain of the diamond industry demonstrate that NGOs can be extremely influential. Tiffany & Co., at first subject to criticism, learned to change its ways and became a leader of the conflict diamond movement. The Kimberley Process demonstrates that NGOs can create change while working with corporations. However, the degree of change, or true goals of the program, may differ in the perspectives of the collaborating organizations.

Notes

1 L. Glendinning, "Diamonds whose price is measured in blood: Jewelers ignore codes of conduct on gems from conflict zones," *The Guardian* October 18 (2004).
2 M. Schuerman, "Behind the glitter: Tiffany and Co. moves to get African 'conflict diamonds' out of its stores," *Stanford Social Innovation Review* Fall (2004), 58.
3 Global Witness, *Déjà vu: Diamond Industry still Failing to Deliver on Promises* (Washington, DC: Amnesty International and Global Witness, 2004).
4 Global Witness, *Déjà vu*.
5 Global Witness, *Déjà vu*.
6 Center for Public Integrity, "Conflict diamonds are forever," November 8 (2002), available at www.globalpolicy.org/security/issues/diamond/2002/1108forever.pdf.
7 Oxfam, "Valentine's gold jewelry sales generate 34 million tons of mine waste," February 11 (2005), available at www.oxfamamerica.org/news andpublications/press_releases/press_release.2005–02–11.6113995793/? searchterm=Tiffany.
8 De Beers, "Diamond best practice principles" (2005), available at www. debeersgroup.com/debeersweb/About+De+Beers/De+Beers+Value+ and+Culture/What+are+BPPs+supporting.htm.
9 Center for Public Integrity, "Conflict diamonds are forever."
10 Diamond Development Initiative, "Diamond development initiative begins," August 15 (2005), available at www.globalpolicy.org/security/ issues/diamond/2005/0815ddi.htm.
11 Diamond Development Initiative, "Diamond development initiative begins."
12 N. D. Innocenti, "Accord on 'conflict diamond' smuggling," *Financial Times* November 15 (2005), available at www.globalpolicy.org/security/issues/diamond/2005/1115smuggling.htm.

Case illustration: Unilever in Indonesia

In the mid-2000s, Unilever Corporation engaged with Oxfam to explore and document the impact of Unilever's presence in Indonesia on poverty and development. Oxfam GB, Novib (Oxfam Netherlands), Unilever and Unilever Indonesia (UI) collaborated on this research project which explored the link between international business and poverty reduction. In particular, the report detailed the positive and negative effects that UI had on poverty in Indonesia. This joint research project resulted in a comprehensive report that has been widely disseminated and is viewed by many as an important example of objective and sincere exploration of the impact of a multinational on the host country in which it does business.

UI, which was founded in 1933, had $984 million in sales by 2003. The majority (84 percent) of sales were derived from home and personal care products, such as soap powder, household cleaning products, soaps and shampoos. The remaining sales were generated from foods such as tea, margarine and ice cream. UI ranks as the thirteenth largest company in Indonesia by sales, and the fourth largest in the fast-moving consumer goods (FMCG) sector. Based on Unilever estimates, at least 95 percent of Indonesians use one or more UI products annually, while 90 percent of poor people in Indonesia buy UI products yearly.[1] Approximately half of Indonesia's population makes less than $2 per day. Marketing to people in poverty presents a number of challenges. Oxfam and UI agreed that items sold should represent good value for money, or serve poverty-related social or environmental goals. More research needs to be done to determine if UI is fulfilling these requirements.

Oxfam believes that the private sector can spur development and be "pro-poor." Foreign direct investment can bring wealth creation, employment and technology transfer. Barbara Stocking, the Director of Oxfam GB, believes that, "Companies, when they act responsibly, can play a vital role in contributing to sustainable development and poverty reduction."[2]

The collaborative research initiative between Oxfam and Unilever set out to explore the tangible effects of Unilever's programs to those living in poverty. As a result of the study and rigorous dialogue, Oxfam believes that they raised Unilever's awareness of their impacts and opportunities.

Some were surprised that a multinational corporation working in developing nations was willing to invite in and provide an NGO like Oxfam an inside look at their organization. However, it was the constant communication and trust that developed between the organizations that helped the collaborative effort to be successful. The trust "enabled [the relationship] to probe deep-seated preconceptions on both sides and explore sometimes painful perceptions of the reality of business operations."[3]

Unilever agreed to work with Oxfam on the report because it recognized that its business was heavily engaged with poor people around the world as both producers and consumers. Also, Unilever considered the Millennium and Johannesburg Declarations, which place poverty eradication as the focal point for global strategies for sustainable development. Unilever wanted to understand the impact of its business operations on poor people in order to know how to support the declarations. Unilever admits that its opinions do not always coincide with Oxfam, and some of its managers were uncomfortable under scrutiny, but they are open to dialogue.

The research documented that UI has had a great impact on development in Indonesia, both positively and negatively. UI has paid a great deal of taxes to the government, employs many workers and has shared best practice standards with the local economy. On the other hand, participation in UI's value chain does not guarantee improvements in the lives of people living in poverty and a debate still exists over what constitutes reasonable performance standards.

The scales may be tipping in UI's favor as the report indicated an estimated 5,000 workforce consisting of 60 percent direct employees and 40 percent contract workers. Furthermore, the company paid its entry-level employees a salary 123 percent of the minimum wage, spent $254 million on supplies purchased mainly from Indonesian distributers and retained nearly $182 million in pre-tax profits annually to reinvest in local business activities. These investments, coupled with the $130 million in annual taxes paid to the government, indicate a commitment to the local economy which will potentially yield positive results for the community. The most notable effort by UI was recognized in 2005 when it received an Energy Globe award for sustainability in the water category.[4] UI is attempting to aid the country against the depleting water supply due to dumping areas that leak into waterways. Efforts have included encouraging the separation of garbage and providing containers where people can compost organic waste, reducing overall dumping.

Notes

1 J. Clay, "Exploring the links between international business and poverty reduction: A case study of Unilever in Indonesia," *Oxfam GB, Novib Oxfam Netherlands, and Unilever* (2005), available at http://oxfam. intelli-direct.com/e/d.dll?m=234&url=http://www.oxfam.org.uk/ what_we_do/issues/livelihoods/downloads/unilever.pdf.
2 Clay, "Exploring the links."
3 Clay, "Exploring the links."
4 www.energyglobe.info/geg/frontend_en/view.php?MENUEID=79. Accessed December 27, 2007.

Case illustration: microfinance and poverty reduction

Financial institutions have provided low-income individuals with small loans for decades. The explosion of microfinance institutions (MFIs) during this period constitutes a significant shift in the international development community.[1] Microfinance initiatives have been implemented as a way to curb poverty, promote community-based development and make a profit. In some instances, the objectives are mutually exclusive, and the cost of making a profit rests on the poverty-stricken in the form of high interest rates. These rates, for the most part, must be high in order for the loaning institution to cover the transfer costs incurred when making many small loans as opposed to a few large loans.[2] Certain poverty-stricken areas could also pose a significant risk to the lending company, deterring them from erecting a branch and increasing costs of loan delivery. Overall, these costs could contribute to the dynamic of the rich getting richer as the poor dive deeper into poverty. This does not seem to be a universal trend, as the microfinance movement received worldwide recognition when Muhammad Yunis, considered the founder of microfinance, was awarded the Nobel Peace Prize in 2006.

Microfinance can attribute its success in the developing world to the nonexistent, weak or exclusionary financial markets. Formal credit systems have a short-sighted reach, providing access to only 1–2 percent of the developed world population.[3] This leaves room for opportunities in the microfinance sector, as a majority of the loans are paid back due to a high return on investment in microenterprises. The returns are a reflection of low labor and infrastructure costs, and the propensity for informal sectors to have lax tax systems and legal costs associated with small businesses created through microfinance loans.[4] Such has been the case in India, where many poor women have been approved for microloans and subsequently built successful businesses. These efforts have resulted in a more than 95 percent repayment rate, statistics that surpass some of the best commercial banks in the world.[5] Despite the explosion of micro-finance providers, economists estimate that less than 5 percent of microenterprise areas such as Latin America have access to institutional sources of credit.[6]

The underserved and potentially far-reaching networks of the microfinance market can provide profits to traditional banks.[7] Collaboration between NGOs and commercial banks seemed appropriate due to complementary resources. Microfinance NGOs demonstrated a propensity towards high returns, and provided services that were in high demand in certain areas. Banks, on the other hand, have access to resources which promote innovation in products, services, advanced technology and development and implementation of market strategies.[8] This includes marketing campaigns during times of rising competition, slowing growth rates, greater demand for new services and the need to expand or simply maintain customer populations.[9] Some institutions can even comply with certain client needs that allow for a grasp on a larger scope of a niche market. For example, Banco Solidario has developed a program that grants immediate loans to individuals who use gold jewelry as collateral.[10]

ACCION International is typically an international partner NGO, such that its presence is not necessarily country-specific. Instead, it can partner with domestic or local NGOs, or for-profit microfinance institutions to provide support in the technical, financial or networking realms. In the case of its relationship with Citibank, it seems as though the larger financial institution provided the growth and networking assistance. Citibank originally was a donor to ACCION programs, and had considered entering the microfinance business through expansion of the company. In lieu of attempting to attract a new customer base, Citibank simply provided more support to ACCION and affiliated NGOs, suggesting that microloan customers become Citibank customers once loans, business checking or other services were upgraded. This allowed ACCION to continue performing the legwork while gaining resources, and for Citibank to inadvertently recruit new customers with little effort.

Another collaboration recently occurred among Grameen Foundation in the US, Citicorp Finance in India, IFMR Trust and Grameen Capital India (GCI) to provide low-interest loans to the poor populations in India. Until microfinancing became legal, GCI was a necessary non-banking financial vehicle to stimulate the stagnant economies inherent in impoverished areas. Currently, about $2 billion is available to the microfinance institutions, but it is estimated that nearly $50 billion is needed, especially since the goal by 2012 is that these microfinance efforts reach at least 100 million households.[11]

Aside from directly contributing to NGOs, large multinational corporations such as MasterCard are partnering with microfinance NGOs to offer financial services such as cash advances and payments through ATMs. In other words, microfinance NGOs provide the larger companies with an abundance of local knowledge and reach. Collaboration can lead to the alleviation of poverty through NGO involvement in credit screenings, social mobilization towards linking households and the larger financial market, and providing skills and enterprise development services which will lead to greater profits and resources for the NGO, the commercial enterprise and the community at large.

Notes

1 M. Berger, "Microfinance: An emerging market within the emerging market," in L. Sawers, D. Schydlowsky and D. B. Nickerson (eds.), *Emerging Financial Markets* (Singapore: Regal Press, 2000), pp. 61–90.

2 V. Akula, "Microfinance boosts the poor," *BusinessWeek Online*, available at www.businessweek.com/debateroom/archives/2007/12/micro-finance_b.html. Accessed December 27, 2007.

3 J. H. Carr and Z. Y. Tong (eds.), *Replicating Microfinance in the United States* (Washington, DC: Woodrow Wilson Center Press, 2002).

4 Akula, "Microfinance boosts the poor."

5 S. Rai, "Tiny loans have big impact on poor," *The New York Times* April 12 (2004), available at http://query.nytimes.com/gst/fullpage.html?res=9D04E0DC1138F931A25757C0A9629C8B63&sec=&spon=&pagewanted=1. Accessed December 27, 2007.

6 Berger, "Microfinance: An emerging market," 61–90.

7 R. P. Christen and R. Rosenberg, "The rush to regulate: Legal frameworks for microfinance," *CGAP Occasional Paper* 4 (2000), Consultative Group to Assist the Poorest.

8 A. M. Rugman and J. P. Doh (eds.), *Multinationals and Development* (New Haven: Yale University Press, 2008).

9 N. Tran, "Marketing in microfinance institutions," *Development Alternatives* Technical Note, no. 2 (2000).

10 Christen and Rosenberg, "The rush to regulate."

11 "Grameen, Citicorp, IFMR form NBFC: CGI will act as an investment banker to MFIs," *Business Standard* January 14 (2008), 2.

PART IV

The future of corporate–NGO relations

9 | The future of corporate–NGO relations

Corporate–NGO relations are increasingly complex, variegated and multifaceted. In this brief final chapter, we review some of the contributions of this book, suggest some implications for researchers and practitioners, and propose some questions and unresolved areas for future attention. We also offer our assessment of the broader trends and trajectories in corporate–NGO interactions from the perspective of co-evolutionary theory.

The continuing progression of NGOs and their strategies

In Chapter 1, we argued that many NGOs now fall in to the "hybrid" category in that they engage in both advocacy and service delivery. Yet, the "radical" advocacy organizations documented in Section II of the book persist and are, perhaps, on the rise. Indeed, one of the more interesting trends to watch is the rise in the more militant NGOs. Al-Qaeda may be viewed as one of the most influential NGOs on the planet today – a pure "advocacy" NGO in the extreme – and Hezbollah, acting as both an "advocacy" and "service" NGO, has grown in the presence of the failed Lebanese state from militant NGO to a pseudo-state player.[1]

These observations suggest, in turn, that our definitions and classifications of NGOs may need to be broadened. For example, are the various militias in Iraq also NGOs? To the extent that this sort of NGO fills a particular political or societal void, it raises serious questions about our understanding of institutional voids. For example, are failed states (Palestine) an extreme form of institutional void that generate an extreme form of NGO (Hezbollah)? Recent research on Jihad has positioned the movement as a global network not dissimilar from the global networks of more conventional NGOs we have documented here.[2]

In Chapter 2 and throughout the book, we have documented the rapid growth in the number of NGOs, the scope of their activities and their power and influence. Will these trends continue? The broad trends toward constrained government expenditures, privatization of public services and pressures from globalization would suggest that service and hybrid NGOs will continue to grow in number and influence. One of the developments likely to fuel this trend is the rapid growth in private foundations that seek to integrate the innovative capability of the private sector with the service delivery of nonprofits to provide a more effective and impactful set of tools to tackle poverty, health and environmental protection. The Bill and Melinda Gates Foundation is a quintessential illustration of this. The Gates Foundation, with more than $33 billion in assets, is increasingly directing its investments to NGOs – both global and local. One program supports a World Health Organization venture with an Indian vaccine maker to sell a meningitis vaccine in Africa for far less than existing vaccines.[3] Other foundations, such as Skoll, Schwab and Google's in-house private philanthropic investment are also taking these innovative approaches to social and environmental development around the world.

Indeed, social innovation and social entrepreneurship, which emphasize the integration of economic and social goals and returns, have gained considerable traction in the world of philanthropy and corporate citizenship more broadly. Social entrepreneurs are being increasingly recognized for the varied and valuable contributions they make to society. These entrepreneurs offer creative solutions to complex and persistent social problems through the adoption of traditional business models. While some believe social entrepreneurship offers an important alternative to entrepreneurial greed and selfishness, others view it as an illusive concept that has been applied indiscriminately to a variety of practices.

Social ventures often leverage private capital or expertise with the resources of NGOs, although in some instances such ventures are pursued purely by a nonprofit or corporate. The Grameen Bank, founded by Mohammed Yunis, is often held up as an example of how innovative approaches can bring radical change to social development by leveraging private sector vehicles (in this case, microfinance) for social benefit.[4] But there are many other instances in which NGOs borrow from corporate practices to initiate innovative and entrepreneurial approaches to their mission, and corporations leverage their intrinsic entrepreneurial orientation to address social problems. Increasingly, social initiatives integrate these two orientations.[5]

Advocacy NGOs, on the other hand, face several potential constraints. First, donors and contributors may be increasingly reluctant to contribute to "pure" advocacy NGOs given the trend described above. Further, increased scrutiny of NGOs and calls for greater accountability and transparency may not work to the advocacy NGOs' advantage. In addition, there may be a backlash against the most extreme tactics of radical NGOs which appears to be prompting some more radical NGOs such as Greenpeace to moderate their tactics.

Another set of related trends which we touched on in Chapters 2 and 8 is the emergence of NGOs from developing countries, the globalization of NGOs and the increasing interactions between MNCs and NGOs in developing counties. As emerging markets grow and develop economically and politically, we expect NGOs in those markets to flourish, and for more liaisons and relationships between and among emerging markets' NGOs and their developed country and global counterparts. We also anticipate that the institutional and ethical complexity detailed in Chapter 2 will only increase the demand for – and growth of – NGO activity around the world.

In terms of the dynamics of corporate–NGO relations, which is the principle focus of the book, we believe that there is a broader evolutionary process underway which we detail below.

Corporate–NGO relations: an evolutionary perspective

Recent research on the co-evolution of organizations and their environment has often highlighted the new organizational forms that emerge from this adaptation process. Indeed, research on strategic adaptation and change has focused closely on the emergence of new organizational forms.[6] Research on new organizational forms illustrates the interrelated nature of strategy and structure. In this case, "forms" is generally interpreted as new structures, but may also refer to strategies or both. Indeed, one view of these organizational forms views them as strategic choices among different configuration options. The traditional boundary of the organization also sought to delineate who is "inside" and who is "outside," and thus helped set the boundary of the firm. While legal boundaries are fundamental, such a narrow conceptualization has limitations for managerial purposes.

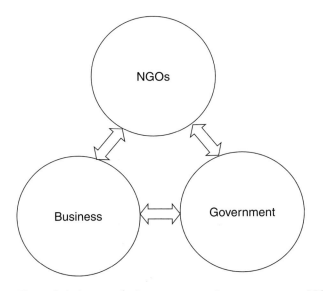

Figure 9.1 A co-evolutionary perspective on corporate–NGO–government relations

Indeed, the managerial boundary of the organization and the legal boundary are frequently different, setting up the conceptual underpinnings of new organizational forms and structures.

In this context, we see the structure and nature of corporate–NGO–government interactions as co-evolutionary; that is changes in one of these three sectors prompt responses which, in turn, generate changes in others. This ongoing, dynamic and interactive set of relationships is depicted in Figure 9.1.

Further, we see a more specific evolution in corporate–NGO relations from discrete, conflictual and isolated interactions to more integrated and embedded exchanges. We see this at both the individual NGO–firm dyad level and more broadly across the totality of NGO–firm relationships.

Stage 1: Conflictual campaigns

In the past, many social purpose NGOs focused a great deal of their conflictual campaigns on firms and industries that they saw as particularly "bad." However, as noted above, there are likely reasons why these campaigns have reached something of a natural limit. First, they lose their novelty over time (e.g., Greenpeace dinghies in front of whaling ships no longer get much coverage). Second, there is only so much attention these campaigns can get and people are at their limits in terms of demands on their attention. Third, big brand firms are becoming more sophisticated in their efforts to pre-empt and/or respond to campaigns, as we have documented throughout the book. Often, these big brand firms are not the "dirty" ones of an industry, but tend to have greater incentive (motive) and resources to ensure that they are relatively clean. Small brand firms need not be especially worried about being targeted, at least on a national or international level.

In sum, campaigning NGOs have to put more and more of their limited resources to fight for a limited amount of attention, having less novelty on their side, working against firms that are tougher targets (in terms of both how "evil" they can plausibly be portrayed to be and how strong they are in their responses). And, if they are successful at the end of such a resource-intensive campaign, they have little ability to shape the final firm behavior and, *most critically*, they will have only changed the behavior of one of the cleaner big brand firms. The rest of the industry, especially the smaller brand firms, will continue in their "dirty" ways.

Stage 2: Partnering with single firms around the firm's practices

Given this, it is not surprising that many NGOs have moved toward partnering. This seems, at least at first blush, a more reasonable way of getting firms – especially big brand firms – to move. The big brand firms are anxious to polish their corporate citizenship credentials and are therefore relatively receptive – even proactive – in seeking out and developing these partnerships. However, in the end, NGOs have often found these partnerships to be quite resource intensive. And, in terms of outcomes, the change on the ground is really often of a single relatively "clean" firm getting marginally cleaner.

Stage 3: Voluntary industry standards

The next natural step, then, has been the rise of efforts toward voluntary industry-wide standards. These efforts have naturally arisen from both a new-found comfort with working with firms, as well as a frustration concerning the amount of effort that needs to be put in if the NGO only works with single firms, and relatively clean ones at that. Clearly the NGOs need to change the whole industry. Firms, wanting to avoid mandatory and perhaps sub-optimal regulation, are also interested in developing these standards as a substitute for potential regulation.

In reality, efforts to develop industry-wide standards have also been very labor-intensive for NGOs, which are often relatively resource-poor. The number of well-established voluntary industry standards that have been created out of such partnerships is likely less than a dozen.

Furthermore, in addition to being very labor intensive to create and fraught with potential failure in their creation, these standards need monitoring and lack enforcement. Viable business models need to be established to ensure monitoring, given that the NGOs that originally create the standards often, at the time the standards are created, themselves lack the resources to monitor firms across the globe. Furthermore, beyond monitoring, these standards are voluntary and thus there are no strong enforcement mechanisms (beyond naming and shaming). And again NGOs face the problem of the small-brand and relatively dirty firms who are less likely to engage in the creation of the standards and also have less incentive to abide by the standards. So, NGOs, in trying to create voluntary standards, face tremendous resource drains in the creation of these standards, with risk of failure, dubious future monitoring and virtually no enforcement against the "dirtiest" players anyway.

Stage 4: The future – collaboration in the creation of new regulations

Given the frustration with voluntary industry-wide standards, many advocacy NGOs seem to be moving to regulation as a means of achieving their goals. In personal conversations with staff of Oxfam, Greenpeace and WWF, and labor rights groups, we have increasingly heard the refrain that they are likely to move toward more of a focus on regulation.

Interestingly, it is in both the interest of NGOs and businesses to work together on shaping regulation. Each alone or in coalitions of their own type (industry groups or NGO coalitions) represents a narrow range of the interests of any given legislator. As such, their lobbying efforts are relatively ineffective compared to broader-based coalitions that include both business interests as well as the interests represented by advocacy NGOs. From the corporation's standpoint, such partnerships are not only much more likely to be successful in shaping the regulatory environment, but they offer a real opportunity for building competitive advantage through nonmarket competition.

All firms operate in a multidimensional regulatory environment, with hundreds of regulations applying to them. Most firms will further exceed regulatory requirements on some dimension or other (e.g., they produce less CO_2 or less mercury or have tighter safety standards, etc.). Ideally – especially since these higher standards might be associated with higher costs – they would like the regulatory standard to be just below their current practices. This would impose additional costs (e.g., retrofitting smokestacks) on their competitors. If they work alone to lobby for such regulation they are unlikely to be especially influential, with competitors and perhaps NGOs in opposition. If, instead they try to raise the regulatory requirements through an industry lobbying group, the representatives within the lobbying group would not accept to put their firms at a competitive disadvantage. Furthermore, a lobbying group will not be hugely influential in shaping legislation because it still only represents a narrow constituency. Thus this approach is unlikely to be realized and, if realized, is unlikely to provide competitive advantage.

If, however, the firm joins with a broad range of NGOs to craft a piece of legislation to lobby around, they are likely to be quite effective in their pressure because of the broad array of constituencies that they represent (e.g., business interests, labor interests, environmental interests). While the firm favor a piece of legislation that would require practices that are just in alignment with the firm's current practices, the partner NGOs will likely push for even higher standards. However, since the firm is one of the parties shaping the legislation, it will be in a position to push for higher standards that will not be unduly costly for it to meet.

This approach thus has a high likelihood of success – because of the broad range of constituencies behind it – and also provides an opportunity for competitive advantage through imposing costs on competitors. Furthermore, there may well be significant reputational

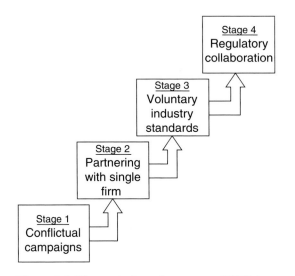

Figure 9.2 The evolution of corporate–NGO interactions

benefits as the firm is not merely partnering to, say, report on or clean its own environment footprint (which is increasingly becoming a non-differentiating hygiene factor), but is actually working with NGOs to raise enforceable standards on the entire industry.

Figure 9.2 summarizes this progression.

Conclusion

NGOs exist – and will likely persist – as an important and influential organizational form within the broader civil society. Corporations, although a relatively new organizational form, appear to be firmly embedded in most modern societies. Moreover, the blurring of organizational boundaries we identified at the beginning of this chapter, and described above in the form of corporate–NGO collaboration to develop new regulation, suggests that corporations and NGOs will interact with increasing frequency, intensity and, potentially, with greater creativity and innovativeness. We believe that these interactions are important, relevant and vital to a thriving social and business sector, and worthy of study and analysis for years to come.

Notes

1 H. Teegen, J. P. Doh and S. Vachani, "The importance of nongovernmental organizations (NGOs) in global governance and value creation: An international business research agenda," *Journal of International Business Studies* 35 (6) (2004), 463–483.

2 See M. Sagemen, *Leaderless Jihad: Terror Networks in the Twenty-First Century* (Philadelphia: University of Pennsylvania Press, 2008).

3 R. A. Guth, "Bill Gates Issues Call For Kinder Capitalism," *Wall Street Journal* January 24 (2008), A1.

4 See A. Counts, *Give us Credit* (New York: Times Books, 1996); D. Bornstein, *The Price of a Dream* (New York: Simon & Schuster, 1996); D. Bornstein, *How to Change the World: Social Entrepreneurs and the Power of New Ideas* (Oxford: Oxford University Press, 2004); J. Elkington and P. Hartigan, *The Power of Unreasonable People: How Social Entrepreneurs Create Markets that Change the World* (Cambridge: Harvard Business School Press, 2008).

5 J. A. Pearce III and J. P. Doh, "The high impact of collaborative social initiatives," *Sloan Management Review* 46 (2) (2005), 30–39.

6 A. Y. Lewin and M. Koza, "Empirical research in co-evolutionary processes of strategic adaptation and change: The promise and the challenge," *Organization Studies* 22 (6) (2001), 5–12; A. Y. Lewin and H. W. Volberda, "Prolegomena on coevolution: A framework for research on strategy and new organizational forms," *Organization Science* 10 (5) (1999), 519–534; H. W. Volberda and A. Y. Lewin, "Co-evolutionary dynamics within and between firms: From evolution to co-evolution," *Journal of Management Studies* 40 (2003), 2111–2136.

Index